BABY CODE

How to Connect with your Baby in your First Year Together

BABY CODE

How to Connect with your Baby in your First Year Together

Dr Silvia Longo

foulsham

LONDON • NEW YORK • TORONTO • SYDNEY

W. Foulsham & Co. Ltd
for Foulsham Publishing Ltd
The Old Barrel Store, Drayman's Lane, Marlow, Bucks SL7 2FF

Foulsham books can be found in all good bookshops and direct from www.foulsham.com

ISBN: 978-0-572-04431-2

A CIP record for this book is available from the British Library

Typeset in Great Britain by Chris Brewer Origination
Printed in Great Britain by Latimer Trend

Contents

Introduction 7

Chapter 1: Understanding Your Baby 9

Chapter 2: The First Six Months.. 29

Chapter 3: 6–12 Months 61

Chapter 4: How Your Baby Can Help You 93

Appendix: Baby Psychology 101 113

Index 123

Introduction

We play during our daily working lives much more than we would comfortably admit to our employers. We play when, during a meeting, we wander off, exchange glances with a colleague or tell a joke to break the ice. We play when we dress up for dinner to impress our guests or when we look for the funny side of things to console ourselves. We play when we flirt with someone or when we pretend to be interested in a serious conversation that we do not care about. But we play like a baby when we are enthralled by a novel, explore a new idea, listen to a piece of music or get lost in a painting. In fact, whenever we are able to contemplate something beautiful, new or interesting, we get closer to the world of babies.

As a parent or caregiver, you can learn more from your baby than you can teach them, and through dedicating your time to playing like a baby you will also develop yourself. This gateway to the infant world offers a unique opportunity for adults to retrieve some of their lost instincts, intuition, creativity and youth. You may become better at managing emotions, being creative, using feelings as a guide, taking risks, or adapting to limited resources or tricky situations.

Most parenting literature describes games as tools to make children smarter and improve a range of skills, from emotional intelligence to hand-eye coordination. This book is different. I focus on playing without an educational goal in mind, showing you how to apply a playful approach to life with your baby in a way that will foster your child's development in all areas. Unlike educational play, playing like a baby is about creating a special time where actions are not necessarily purposeful, useful or goal oriented; where the pace is slow, attention is paid to small and ordinary things, nothing is considered meaningless and every exploration is worth pursuing. Time spent in this way will in turn provide you with vital refreshment, as well as feeding your baby's mind with the nourishment it needs. You will also deepen your bond and find contentment – the most effective antidote for our society's obsession with performance, competition and the pursuit of high standards.

Many mothers have said to me over the years that just as they felt their interactions with their babies were becoming more meaningful, it was time to go back to work. I hope that this book will help new parents to make the most out of a very short time – the baby's first year – and enjoy it to the full.

Chapter 1

Understanding Your Baby

Babies are complex creatures. To understand some of the challenges that can arise in a relationship with them, try to imagine the following task. You must sit for an afternoon with someone who does not speak your language, or any language you understand. They do not know what you do, nor are they interested in finding out. They have interests of their own but you don't understand them. They often look at you as if wanting something, but you can only guess what it might be. You are expected to be in control and to make this person happy. So, how would you feel about such a task?

Understanding your baby can take some time and I hope that this book will help you along the way. However, your baby understands *you* better than you might think. Because they do not know the meaning of words, babies relate to the aspects of ourselves that are more *real* – they are not easily deceived by the front we put up for others. They will evaluate your tone of voice, manner of speaking, eye contact and posture, as well as the consistency between your words and actions (i.e. sounding confident but looking nervous). Although language takes over to an extent, we still rely on this information as adults; for example, have you ever met someone and immediately felt that you couldn't trust them? It is instincts such as these which suggest that we have a deep-rooted blueprint of baby feelings and emotions which go on to influence many of our experiences as adults.

In this chapter I will be offering you insight into the world of a baby (further information can also be found in the age-specific chapters). By getting on board with your baby's thoughts and feelings, you will be better equipped to interact with them. This will develop your bond immeasurably and help you to feel more confident and capable in your role as a loving parent.

Your baby's abilities

All of us have wondered, at some point, just how well a baby understands what is going on around them. In the past babies were seen as relatively helpless, but that picture is now fading as researchers are discovering more and more evidence to suggest that babies are much more competent than we have given them credit for. It now seems that a basic understanding of feelings, intentions and behaviour is present from the first few weeks, to an extent that was previously deemed impossible.

This does not mean that you shouldn't discuss anything in front of your baby other than jolly matters and the weather. It is helpful, however, to keep in mind that your child, at whatever age, goes through the same experiences as you, only in an indirect way: they share your world and are affected by it. By recognising that your child is a switched-on member of your family, who constantly takes things on board, you help them to make sense of all the good, bad and ordinary events that unfold before their eyes.

It is well worth talking to your baby to involve them wherever you can. Although they do not yet understand language, your baby will appreciate your effort to help them make sense of what is going on around them. Your words may not have a magical effect, but your baby will certainly understand that you are addressing them to offer explanations and reassurance; at the very least they will enjoy your spoken attention! If they do not like what they are hearing or are not interested they will soon let you know – they will divert their gaze, direct their attention elsewhere, or even loudly protest and talk over you.

Even though the precise extent of babies' understanding is yet to be established, it is better to assume that they are competent and aware rather than believing they are oblivious to what is going on around them. There are various reasons why this is the case:

Firstly, if you adopt the 'competent baby' view you will naturally protect your newborn from unnecessary stress, such as allowing them to witness a heated argument.

Secondly, if you assume that babies somehow understand your communications through non-verbal channels and instinct, you will feel much more motivated to spend your time interacting and playing with them. You will also find your ordinary chit-chat with them becomes much more interesting; peppered with explanations, consolations, tales and promises.

Finally, by regarding your baby as an intelligent, understanding creature, you will naturally also treat them with the respect, consideration and mindful attention they deserve.

Your baby's emotional life

Putting feelings into words is the first step towards becoming emotionally intelligent. It requires paying attention to emotions arising in yourself or another person, recognising them and giving them a name. So what is a baby's emotional life like? Are a baby's feelings comparable to ours?

There are numerous theories, but psychoanalysts Wilfred Bion and Donald Winnicott focus on the relationship between mother and child. They explain how simply putting a newborn's confused emotions into words can help them to develop a mind of their own, recognising and transforming their feelings and instincts. However, since nobody has yet managed to interview a baby or to record their thoughts, this leaves us with a lot of guessing to do when it comes to recognising a baby's feelings and putting them into words for them.

Although not exhaustive, here is a list of the feelings and emotions that your baby may plausibly experience:

Tired	Contented	Frustrated
Hungry	Excited	Angry
Thirsty	Curious	Upset
Satiated	Sense of Accomplishment	Afraid
Pain	Secure	Restless
Uncomfortable	Insecure	Settled
Unsettled	Impatient	Relieved

You can help your baby to recognise and handle feelings simply by pointing them out, using your own intuition and experience as a guide. When you spend time with your child, whether actively playing or simply being together, you can naturally comment on what their physical or emotional state seems to be. If they cry, you may comment on how hungry/tired/in pain they seem to be, offering a few soothing words to make them feel better. Voicing such impressions is very straightforward; for example: 'This tummy must be empty!' or 'This is exciting, isn't it?' Although your baby will not know the meaning of each single word, they will understand your overall communications and know exactly what you are talking about long before they can speak.

Tip: Making similar comments whenever the same situation repeats itself is particularly useful, as it establishes a kind of 'emotional routine' that can be helpful in overcoming challenges and obstacles.

Putting feelings into words can have so many advantages, not just for baby but for you too. Talking about feelings helps you to keep things in perspective and to avoid the build-up of emotion that can sometimes lead you to overreact to something quite minor. Sharing your own emotions with your baby is going to make your relationship more rewarding, strengthening your bond and understanding of one another.

Avoid testing your baby's progress

Psychological testing has been part of my job for many years and like many of my colleagues, I do not particularly enjoy it! Although we are trying to accurately measure a child's abilities, part of us secretly hopes for great results, just as a parent would – especially if that child is eager to do well. Being tested is a stressful task even when you know you are competent, because the moment you are formally examined you rely upon an expert's verdict to confirm whether your positive view of yourself is justified. The same applies to your view of your child when they are being tested. However, you should not trust a test's results above your own judgement – doing so is likely to feed your insecurity and possibly your child's, with no real gain.

As a parent, you may think that you are never in the same position as a psychologist administering a test. But how many times have you compared your baby's progress to that of other infants? How many times have you lined up a series of coloured balls and asked which one is red/green/yellow? How often have you tested your baby's understanding of language by asking them to give you the ball/the elephant/the truck? I bet it's a fair few times. It's fine to observe progress in your child but unless you have real concerns about your baby's development (in which case you need to seek professional advice) 'testing' your baby during the course of your daily interactions is best avoided.

How your child compares to others, and whether or not they are above or below average in their development is not relevant to their current or future happiness. Even though a child with exceptional skills makes their parents deliriously proud, we've all seen cases of child prodigies whose extraordinary talents have actually hindered success and fulfilment in their adult lives.

Of course, we all want our children to be clever and most of us regard intelligence as a key to success. However, numerous studies have shown that personality and outlook on life are far better predictors of happiness and success than educational accomplishments, economic status and career planning. In fact, optimism, enthusiasm, and positive emotions in general are not only vital to happiness and success but to health and longevity too. Therefore, we should really concern ourselves with giving our babies the best start in life by providing emotional security, warmth and positive attention and by not worrying about performance – something that playing like a baby aims to help you do. As the psychologist Carl Rogers convincingly argued, a baby who receives positive attention whatever they do (unconditional love) is likely to develop a good level of confidence and self-esteem. On the other hand, a baby who is only appreciated when they meet their parents' expectations (conditional love) is more likely to develop a shaky sense of value and grow up feeling that they have to do certain things in order to be likable.

Over time, natural talents will emerge in your child. Although these gifts can be enhanced with training and education, any talent can be cultivated and enjoyed privately for the sheer pleasure of learning, personal development and discovery. The main advantage of these gifts is that they make life a more interesting, enjoyable and satisfying journey, with or without the additional reward of outward success.

Withhold negative judgement

For many months after my first daughter was born I found myself listening to a lot of unhelpful nonsense in the form of advice, with only the occasional tip having any practical use. Like any first-time mother, I was vulnerable and sensitive to judgement, especially when so many people felt entitled to give their opinion on how *my* baby should be dealt with. Since unrequested advice is a glorified form of criticism, I feel justified for feeling irritated (and sometimes downright furious) upon hearing the words 'Why don't you…'

When my daughter was old enough to sit by herself, friends and relatives insisted I got a playpen so she could learn some independence while I got more time to myself. I honestly dislike playpens; I don't like the way they look and I don't like their philosophy. But peer pressure got the better of me and eventually I succumbed to their chorus of suggestions and plonked my daughter in a playpen borrowed from a friend. It was a complete failure from the start – my daughter would start screaming at a terrific volume the minute her bum touched the bottom of that miserable object. Playpen supporters were ready to make not-so-subtle references to my baby being spoilt and in dire need of discipline, but the issue was resolved when I chose to interpret events differently. I decided that in fact it wasn't my daughter being unreasonable – after all, a cage isn't appealing, no matter what you call it.

This shows how your expectations and interpretation of events can make a huge difference to your life. Like my example, you can assume, without any good reason or sound evidence, that your baby should perform at a certain level (i.e. independent behaviour) or should adapt to a certain situation (i.e. playing in a restricted space). But if your child doesn't behave as you anticipated, it is incredibly important that you review your beliefs and expectations. Does it matter if your child does something different from other children? What is the real consequence if they want to be picked up while other babies are managing independently? Admittedly, certain behaviours are less convenient and clinginess can be terribly irritating – at least until you realise that it is a temporary nuisance, and one that has a positive side too. When your baby's need for attention gets in the way, the best thing you can do is throw away your expectations about them (along with the day's to-do list) and simply snuggle up with them.

The importance of positively-framed judgement cannot be overestimated. Think what a difference it makes if you say to yourself that your child *prefers* spending time with you, rather than saying they *need* you because they can't tolerate even a small degree of separation, or worse – that they are spoilt. If your child, like mine, refuses to use the playpen, you are much better off refraining from negative judgement and opting for a more neutral interpretation, such as 'She doesn't like to sit in a confined space on her own' – I challenge anybody to find something wrong with that!

Parents' negatively-framed judgements about their children can be surprisingly varied and imaginative. They can be straightforward (and usually inaccurate) comparisons such as: 'He's not like his brother' (when the sibling is a high achiever) or 'He's just like his father' (somebody in the family who did poorly). They can also be comments referring to physical characteristics (too fat, too skinny, too clumsy), psychological traits (nervous, introverted, obstinate) or behavioural patterns (hyperactive, clingy, manipulative).

Whenever we formulate these judgements, we should be aware of a phenomenon called the 'self-fulfilling prophecy'. Around forty years ago, psychologists Robert Rosenthal and Lenore Jacobson convincingly demonstrated what everyone suspected: our predictions about other people can influence their performance in a way which makes them conform to our expectations.

Rosenthal and Jacobson looked at a primary school register and picked out some names at random. They invented a story to convince the teachers that this group of students was bound to increase their performance in the following months, suggesting that the students were 'late bloomers'. A year passed and they returned to find that the students who had been bestowed with positive expectations had improved significantly compared to their classmates.

The explanation for this finding is relatively simple – no magic, telepathy, or any other extraordinary force was at work. Through their behaviour, the teachers communicated their positive expectations to the children, who in turn felt trusted and appreciated. It is quite possible that these 'late bloomers' were also given more consideration, patience and encouragement, and that any negative results were regarded as below their true potential. The students undoubtedly felt special – something that is bound to produce positive results.

Negative expectations work in the same powerful way, just in the opposite direction. So is it then wise to try and silence our negative, fault-finding voice? Should we cast ourselves and others, especially our children, in the best possible light? In an ideal world one should refrain from any judgement, positive or negative, since all evaluations are only partially correct; however, this is virtually impossible, so framing each and every aspect of your child's characteristics in a realistic, but positive and accepting way will really help both you and your child. This will allow you to truly appreciate your baby's unique personality, and see them for who they really are, rather than the abstract 'ideal child' who, unlike your real, imperfect one, cannot make any contribution to your happiness.

Remember: Every downside has its reverse and, especially in the case of children, what may seem like a disadvantage now may very well turn out to be an advantage in the future.

Bonding through play

Have you ever had to take part in one of those horrific team-building exercises which are meant to break the ice during office training days? If so, you know that there are many games to play which are aimed at helping you to get acquainted with somebody or to see someone you already know in a new light. Playing games is a good personal introduction because it makes social formalities redundant, allowing you to collect a series of impressions about other people without the focus being on getting to know each other.

First-hand observations made during interactions like play are a far better guide to understanding others than observations made from the sidelines – this enables us to get a sense of how someone really is, rather than confirming any preconceived ideas or expectations. This doesn't just apply to formal situations like work; it applies to getting to know your baby too. Playtime without an educational agenda is the best and easiest road to bonding and it is what babies are naturally driven towards. It takes the pressure off the relationship, making both people focus on something external which unites them, entertains them and helps them to get to know each other in a relaxed way. Because play encourages us to drop our fears and inhibitions, each time you play with your child you are giving them opportunities to express themselves freely, developing their confidence and deepening your understanding of each other.

It is useful to keep in mind that the knowledge you build up of your baby through play can be intuitive and not necessarily conscious. This means that you might not be able to put into words all the things you know about your child, even though you have a definite sense of who they are and despite the fact that such instinctive awareness guides you whenever you have to make important decisions. What we call a 'mother's instinct' derives from spending a lot of time caring for a baby, not from giving birth.

Here are some examples of the instinctive knowledge you may have about your child:

- How they tackle new experiences (toys, people, situations) and how long they need to adjust to them

- How resilient they are in the face of obstacles and failure and what their problem-solving strategies are

- To what extent they rely on your guidance

- What their 'cognitive style' is – whether they pay attention to tiny details or prefer to get an overall impression of things

- What their optimum level of activity is

Let's say, for example, that you are playing with your baby, rolling a shiny new ball towards them and waiting for their next move. Do they look at you questioningly for guidance? Do they throw themselves at the ball you rolled or do they take a more cautious approach? Do they taste it? Throw it away? Shake it? Pass it from one hand to the other? Hit the floor with it? Roll it back towards you? Whatever they do will stay in

your memory, stored away with thousands of other images, feeding your instinct and unique understanding of your child.

It may be an obvious truth to say that, in order to build a strong positive bond with your baby, you need to invest your time and resources. One of the great misconceptions about children, which has a strong grasp on the current generation of parents, is that contented babies should be independent and self-entertaining; sadly, it seems that a baby which protests loudly to get your attention and demands a lot of your time is considered to be badly parented. However, as a gifted community nurse once pointed out to me, in too many instances professionals diagnose 'attention-seeking' behaviour and fail to point out the 'attention-needing' aspects of it. I would argue that all children are attention-needing (not just attention-seeking) and at times their needs may seem excessive, especially when they happen to clash with everybody else's.

Children need plenty of social interaction to thrive. If you expect that your baby should happily play by themselves while you do your own things you will probably end up feeling frustrated; no doubt you will also struggle to do what you had planned, due to their presence and loud interruptions. However, if you reduce your expectations and accept that during the first year of your baby's life you will have little spare resources for yourself, you will end up with far fewer inner conflicts, guilty feelings and fears of going wrong, together with a more contented baby. It is therefore the best solution to accept and understand that your baby will need your time and to stop feeling bad about it; if they happen to request a great amount of attention, give it to them – this does not necessarily mean they are spoilt, attention-seeking or over-dependent.

Playing without teaching

Perhaps because of the importance that our culture places on achievement, many people find it difficult to think of playing as an activity in its own right. Days become containers that need to be filled with remunerative activities on one hand and purposeful leisure on the other – never, in any case, to be wasted in idleness. Although the pursuit of a long-term goal may increase *your* motivation to get involved in a range of activities, this is not the case for young children, who by nature enjoy a sense of freedom from restraints and impositions of all sorts.

Structured activities, where you need to follow a series of steps in order to get to an end result, are not suited to a baby's spirit. Playing like a baby is more about refraining from the impulse to teach and train, dropping any agenda you have prepared for your baby to focus on the happenings of the present rather than the goals of the future. Learning happens of its own accord and intelligence develops as a by-product of play and interaction without the need for an active pursuit of it. If your time is spent pleasantly, your baby is entertained and you are not bored or irritated, that is already an achievement.

It can certainly be inspiring to show your baby how to do things, and you may occasionally want to shift the emphasis from the fun aspect of playing to that of learning. However, if you choose an educational attitude as your main communication channel, your child may end up struggling to reach out to you. By the same token, if you are used to wearing the wise teacher's hat, you may struggle to let your child 'console' you when you feel fragile and when a frolicsome giggle with your baby is just what you need.

The psychology: An analysis of the fate of the young musicians who, over the years, won the famous and prestigious International Paganini Prize for violin players, showed that surprisingly few of the winners go on to become outstanding or celebrated performers.

In reporting and explaining this, the Italian psychiatrist Paolo Crepet argues that the same skills that lead you to win such a competitive prize may work against you in other respects. Fear of failure and the need to come first, for example, are not great assets when it comes to playing in an orchestra, where cooperation and willingness to measure yourself against others in a non-competitive way are essential.

Gaining your baby's approval

For months my second daughter shunned a dear friend of our family, possibly due to his brusque manners deriving from his attempt at being funny, together with his ignorance of personal space. This started a vicious cycle – the more he tried to interact with her, the more she would withdraw from him. When she started frowning at the mere sight of him, he eventually gave up trying to make her laugh. In doing so, she then started looking out for him!

This was just a series of minor incidents, which made everybody laugh, but when the person involved is a babysitter, a grandparent or a parent, the repercussions can be more serious. Feelings can be quite badly hurt and the person involved may have their confidence knocked or begin to feel inadequate in some way. This is particularly true of couples going through a difficult time in their relationship, as the baby's 'preference' for one parent can really add to the strain.

Few people openly admit that it is upsetting to have a baby crying in your arms because you are not their mum, but this is extremely common. What does it mean when a child cries as soon as you hold them? Though this might happen with uncanny regularity, it is wrong to assume that you have done something wrong or that the baby simply doesn't like you. With babies, you really need to get down to basics and look at the simple explanations first. A hungry and tired infant will tolerate their discomfort better when they are in their most comfortable and familiar place, while anything new or unfamiliar will not seem such an attractive option.

Before jumping to conclusions about your baby's preferences, try changing simple things like their position or your tone of voice (some people have a natural tendency to bellow). You could also slow down your movements or distract them with an interesting toy. When you don't know what is wrong, it will be impossible to know what will work, so it really will be a case of trial and error. Your baby will be fascinated by your endeavours, if nothing else!

Although it can be upsetting if a baby doesn't respond to you in the way you would like, you must not take it personally. If you have patience, warmth and a genuine interest you already have the essential qualities for a rewarding relationship with your baby.

When things go wrong

As described in the previous section, there will be times when things simply do not work out; there is no clear cause for your baby's discontent and nothing you do seems 'right'. In situations like this, a range of negative emotions can arise, from mild irritation to feelings of helplessness or inadequacy. Unfortunately, this can result in issuing blame, be it on yourself, your baby, or your partner. However, if you can divert this to something external, you will all feel much happier for it. Externalisation channels frustration in a constructive way, enabling you to become more resilient and allowing you to enjoy a more positive frame of mind.

I'll explain further with this case study:

Family therapist Michael White discovered something that helps families whose lives are badly affected by the child's daily 'soiling' incidents, at a time when the milestone of bowel control should be fully reached. He introduced 'Sneaky Poo', a naughty and unruly character whose intolerable behaviour becomes the cause of all the havoc. Sneaky Poo soils bed linen, underwear and trousers. He creates embarrassment, shame and frustration. He spoils parties, day trips and even school days. When he sneaks in everything has to stop until his mess is cleaned up.

A character so apt at attracting disapproval helps children to feel less guilty and more motivated to win the race to the loo (or potty). As they get ready to engage in battle, parents are in a much better position to join in their efforts – the blame game is over.

Of course, Sneaky Poo is not the only one to cause disruption! Other unwanted visitors frequently turn up in the life of a baby, be it the windy colic they suffer in the first three months, or those tiny teeth that begin pushing their way to the surface just as the wind situation was improving. If you can treat these as external nuisances, it will really help.

Tip: Externalisation also works well with accidents. If your baby bumps their head on the edge of a low table they will be frightened, hurt and upset. You will be alarmed and concerned, and may feel guilty for not childproofing the house effectively or for not supervising more closely. It is easy to see how such a simple and common event can create bad feelings and how, just by blaming the table and issuing it a few well-deserved slaps, you can all feel much better!

A different, though equally valid, approach to tackle temporary difficulties is to think that you do not necessarily need to find an explanation at all. Sometimes the cause is harder to see than the solution, so you may find it easier to simply try and fix it. Through this process of trial and error you will also better understand the effect that your actions have on your baby. Don't agonise over what the cause might be – tricky times *always* occur, and it makes sense to accept this, so long as they remain manageable.

Tip: Do something with your baby that is consistent with the mood you are in. If you are bubbly and full of sparkling energy, exciting games will provide great satisfaction all round; but if you are feeling tired and miserable, is peek-a-boo the best activity? How will you manage the smiles and shrieks that normally go with it? Your baby is likely to be confused by the difference between your actions and your real state of mind (which babies will always pick up on). If you're having a bad day or feeling low, read a book, give the baby a bath and a massage, or just attend to them quietly until your low spell is over.

Key points

- Babies relate to the aspects of ourselves that are more *real* – they are not easily deceived by the front we put up for others.

- By getting on board with your baby's thoughts and feelings, you will be better equipped to interact with them, developing your bond immeasurably and helping you to feel more confident and capable in your role as a loving parent.

- Keep in mind that your child, at whatever age, goes through the same experiences as you, only in an indirect way: they share your world and are affected by it.

- Talk to your baby to involve them wherever you can. Although they do not yet understand language, your baby will appreciate your effort to help them make sense of what is going on around them.

- Putting your baby's confused emotions into words can help them to develop a mind of their own. You can help them to recognise and handle feelings simply by pointing them out, using your own intuition and experience as a guide.

- Making similar comments whenever the same situation repeats itself is particularly useful, as it establishes a kind of 'emotional routine' that can be helpful in overcoming challenges and obstacles.

- It is fine to observe progress in your child but unless you have real concerns about your baby's development, 'testing' your baby during the course of your daily interactions is best avoided.

- How your child compares to others and whether or not they are above or below average in their development is not relevant to their current or future happiness.

- Beware of the 'self-fulfilling prophecy': our predictions about other people can influence their performance in a way which makes them conform to our expectations.

- Try to frame your child's characteristics in a realistic, but positive and accepting way. This will allow you to appreciate your baby's unique personality, and see them for who they really are.

- Because play encourages us to drop our fears and inhibitions, each time you play with your child you are giving them opportunities to express themselves freely, developing their confidence and deepening your understanding of each other.

- Structured activities are not suited to a baby's spirit. Playing like a baby is about refraining from the impulse to teach and train, dropping any agenda you have prepared for your baby to focus on the happenings of the present rather than the goals of the future.

- Although it can be upsetting if a baby doesn't respond to you in the way you would like, you must not take it personally. If you have patience, warmth and a genuine interest you already have the essential qualities for a rewarding relationship with your baby.

- Try to externalise – this will channel your frustration in a constructive way. Remember Sneaky Poo!

- Remember: tricky times *always* occur.

- Do something with your baby that is consistent with the mood you are in.

Chapter Two

The First Six Months

In this chapter we will look at what your baby understands in the first six months of their life and how you can deepen your bond through playing like a baby. The activities I will discuss are very broad and although I give specific examples, please don't feel you have to follow them exactly – the idea is that you are inspired to come up with your own games and simply have fun!

The first six months of life are a fascinating time for a variety of reasons, including the fact that very few of us claim to have any memory from this time. There are, however, more and more studies indicating that the earliest months of life, although not remembered, are also not forgotten. During the first two years of life your baby's brain will complete its physical growth and maturation and during this time experiences can leave an indelible mark, even though they may not be directly remembered. Researchers examining the attachment bond between mother and child are suggesting that it is the ordinary, everyday care which you regularly provide for your child that has the most importance in shaping their future development, and not, as you may think, those exceptional but rare events (like the time you got really mad and screamed your head off or that day you took them to Disneyland). Think of it like this: the little drops of water that constantly fall on a particular spot on a rock will eventually cause a dip in the surface of the stone. The deluge, when it is only a freak occurrence, won't produce such lasting consequences.

When your baby is born you have to make room for them. Though they were certainly already in your mind, when you were pregnant, they weren't physically present yet, and it is only from the moment they arrive that you can start to collect your first real impressions of them, see how you can best meet their needs and tentatively initiate your first 'games'. You needn't feel pressured to come up with elaborate activities and expensive toys – this phase is about having quiet and intimate interactions with a tiny person who is completely new to you, and the best games are those that you initiate based on your own observations. Unlike adult pastimes, playing with your baby doesn't need much planning – it is more like a dance where every step is improvised and there is a constant alternation of leading and following (even if it doesn't look that way). It is important for you to remember that preconceived ideas and expectations can often be counterproductive. Nothing is as relevant and important as your own observations in determining what will work for your baby.

Watching your baby

From the very beginning of their life, everything your baby does has a meaning and a purpose. None of the movements or expressions they make are pointless, however small or seemingly insignificant. Paying attention to these details will allow you to fully appreciate and enjoy your baby's daily progress, which, like a murmur in a noisy place, can so easily be missed. Becoming a good observer is not necessarily easy – distinguishing, noticing and remembering small details can be extremely challenging, especially if you are like me (short-sighted and absent-minded). However, being able to accurately and effectively observe the world around you is not a skill that you are either born with or you can forget about: it is something that you can cultivate.

How do you cultivate it? Firstly, you need to believe that there is something to be seen and that it is worth seeing. If the object of your interest is subtle, understated or camouflaged, there is little hope that you will spot it by chance, and even if you do, you will not make much of it. When you watch your baby, it is therefore useful to keep in mind that where they look, how they look, if they smile, where they turn, how they reach out or how they flap their hands are all ways of exploring and communicating, as well as possible reactions to internal states and feelings.

Apart from a few reflexes, everything that you see is unique to your baby, even if it looks a lot like what all other babies do. What you see happening over and over again will give you a good indication of what your baby recognises, prefers, dislikes, finds exciting, tiring and so on. If you pay attention to their non-verbal communications, babies are able, to a certain extent, to guide your behaviour, 'choosing' the activities they prefer. For this purpose, one of the most powerful tools at a baby's disposal is eye contact – by gazing intently in your eyes or looking away, a baby tells you when they want you engaged and when they need to switch off and have quiet time. Unlike the screaming that they perform when they want to be picked up, looking away is a subtle message, and one that you are going to receive through being observant.

To draw pleasure from watching your baby you need patience and passion. Patience is required to withstand those times during which not much is happening (at least not visibly from the outside); passion is necessary to leave important things behind in order to be able to catch the moment your child moves a hand towards an object or smiles for the first time. Cultivating an interest in these details of your child's development is also going to provide you with many more memories from those early months which, according to most people, fly past.

Watching your baby is a wonderful thing to do. When your baby arrives into the world, you only have a biological relationship. You may have premonitions, intuitions or feelings about how they will turn out

to be, but these are often wrong and best left aside to make room for the real impressions coming from how your baby actually is. It is impossible to have it all worked out from the start, or from the first weeks, months or years. If you think you do, you will not observe with your eyes but will just seek confirmation of your expectations. That is why observation is so important. It helps you to learn about your baby and for them to learn about you. You can't know everything right away – don't be afraid to take all the time you need to get to know each other.

The beauty of touch

In the earliest stages of life our 'self' is very much rooted in the body and its functions; so much so that mental and physical functions are sometimes regarded as the same thing. Touch gestures, such as cuddling your baby, stroking their head or holding their hand are therefore the surest ways of reaching out to them, making your presence felt at the level they can best appreciate. These physical interactions have also been found to strengthen babies' immune systems, as well as lowering the risk of developing eczema and other skin problems.

Feeding

Breastfeeding is one of the easiest ways in which you can establish a physical bond with your child. However, when only bottle-feeding is possible, you can still hold your baby in a warm and comfortable position, where giving food is not a 'chore' but a pleasure. Finding a snug position from where you can easily embrace your baby allows you to notice their warm, biscuity smell; hear the soft and loud noises they make and to monitor their reassuring, regular breathing. The repetition of such moments over many weeks and months will give you that 'physical' knowledge of your child that will make your relationship so special. Needless to say, I am not a fan of breastfeeding techniques, such as the so-called 'rugby' position – many of these minimise contact between mother and child, reducing the possibility of cuddling and comforting, making it impossible for the baby to fall asleep in your arms once their tummy is full. Just be close and comfortable.

Massage

Massaging your baby is a natural and instinctive activity that can unwisely be transformed into something to add to your to-do list; something that requires you to attend a course and 'qualify' before you can handle your baby. As long as you are gentle, you don't risk doing any harm to your baby; plus, there is plenty of free advice from health practitioners as well as from parents who have practised it themselves.

Massage can be part of the flow of the day and just one of the ways in which you relate to your baby; you don't necessarily need a special place, time, lighting or atmosphere. Although there is nothing wrong with creating an ambience, to me it feels a bit artificial (and like a lot of unnecessary fuss). It makes much more sense to regard massage as just a form of touching where you take more time, pay more attention to the movements you make and observe the effect they have on your baby. When you hear the loud noise the wind makes as it finally leaves your baby's tummy, you know that your gentle circular clockwise rubbing of their belly – recommended to help relieve colic pain – has done its job. This massage of the tummy is a common one, and there are numerous other ways in which you can introduce massage as part of the daily routine. Think, for example, of nappy changing time. You pop your baby on the changing mat and coo at them while getting everything organised for a swift change. However, you see that their bottom is very red and you are worried they are feeling sore. You put on some soothing cream to help the bottom heal and want to wait a little while before putting the clean nappy on to give the cream a better chance to work. Holding your baby's feet up, you can start moisturising and massaging their legs and when they seem tired you can sit them upright or turn them onto their tummy to start massaging their back. If your baby is very small, it is likely they will have presented you with another wee and, providing nothing is burning in the oven, this will give you another opportunity to start all over again.

It is examples like this that allow you to practise massage with your baby on a daily basis without turning it into a therapy session. Having a mat on the floor in order to sit down comfortably when you need to change them and, when you feel like it, massage them, has the advantage of reducing the risk of falls to zero and allows you to take your time with the necessary grooming (doing things in a rush with babies, including changing nappies, is never a good thing and rarely makes the process much quicker).

Carrying

Whenever you carry your baby as you go out with a friend, walking, shopping or attending to other errands, you establish a physical relationship with them. Tightly secured to your body, your baby learns about your smell, the rhythm of your movements, and the synchrony of your voice and gestures. Baby carriers (slings, pouches or harnesses) also leave your hands free, and unless you need to do heavy shopping, it is far more practical than a pram (although be aware you need to wait several weeks before your baby's back is strong enough to be safe in that position). Initially, your baby must be placed facing you, and from this position you can kiss them on the head, feel their temperature and know whether they are sweating or getting cold. You can also touch, hold and massage their hands and feet, even if they are covered up.

As your baby gets older, you will notice how their engagement with the world steadily increases. From this pouch, feeling secure and protected, your baby will scan their surroundings. Although perhaps only a few things are able to attract their attention in the beginning, over time they progressively react to more subtle stimulation, eventually seeking out favourite objects and selecting their own landscape. Don't be fooled into  thinking your baby will not appreciate art, architecture and nature – their observation skills are keener than you might think. A four-month-old will notice, and even become fond of, certain details that you may have been unaware of, like the features of a street lamp, a stain on a wall or a dent in the side of your car. Although your baby is amenable enough to let you inspire them by guiding their attention, it is useful to remember that from the very beginning they have eyes of their own.

Tip: Does your baby suffer from colic? Carrying them on you is one of the best remedies as when an infant is hanging comfortably from your body, their tummy is also pacified. Your heartbeat and the warmth of your body have a general soothing effect (this is why some babies can't help falling asleep after only the first few gentle swings).

> **Be aware:** Are they starting to twist their neck to get a better picture of things? This is a sure sign your baby is getting ready to face outwards.

Explorations

When my first baby was five months old, I woke up one day thinking of blowing bubbles and realised that my girl must be old enough to enjoy the beautiful impression of lightness and luminosity that they produce. I wasn't wrong, and their charm was clearly reflected in her eyes (becoming her all-time favourite ever since).

To distract or entertain, to pacify or amuse, we always try to attract a baby's attention by parading fancy toys and other objects that we consider appealing, such as our house keys or mobile phone. However, a baby's own independent explorations are often much more subtle, involving things that may appear quite unattractive to us. There is one very clear reason for this: we are not used to looking at our surroundings as if  we had never seen them before. This creates a world of difference between a newborn and us; one that can be bridged by playing like a baby.

Once we become used to our daily landscape we develop a series of blind spots and stop seeing what our eyes absorb. For example, can you picture the front of the house next to yours? What adorns their windowsills? Has anyone changed the flower arrangement in the front garden? Unlike babies, we often don't let our ordinary landscape impress us, even when we could do with a little distraction and stimulation.

Besides colour, shape and size, objects are defined by many other features, including symmetry, contrast, solidity, texture, temperature and so on, and these characteristics can be taken for granted or misunderstood. Think of a snake. They look slimy and wriggly but in fact feel very smooth and muscular. In the way that a snake feels quite different from the way it looks, so do many everyday objects, particularly to a baby. To understand your baby's point of view and their interest in looking, mouthing, touching and grasping, try to touch something with your eyes closed. Running your finger and pressing your lips against any familiar object will give you lots of new information about something you thought you knew pretty well. These new sensations will provide you with an interesting clue as to the amount of discoveries that your baby is busy making every day.

Mouthing

In the first trimester, the favourite investigation tool is the mouth! 'Mouthing' takes the lead in exploration during this period and is by far the preferred method for getting to know the world. The mouth and its connected activities, such as sucking, licking and eating, are all linked to cognitive and psychological development, as they allow the baby to gather information about shape, dimension, texture, temperature, taste and so on.

As we grow older, we can tell just by looking at something whether it is big or small, smooth or rough, soft or hard. However, babies need experience to formulate these simple judgements. A baby doesn't know that a football is too big to be eaten with just one bite, and that is why they will give it a go – only when they have repeated experiences can they learn about relative sizes and proportions.

Although a baby's world is still largely unknown to us, with the little we know we can try to put ourselves in a baby's tiny shoes. Think of objects that are familiar to you, and how they would feel if you put them in your mouth:

- **Keys:** cold, irregular shape, metallic smell, bitter taste

- **Wooden table:** warm, hard, smooth, woody smell, sweet and salty taste

- **Purse:** warm, soft, smooth, leathery smell and taste

All these impressions accumulate in your baby's mind when they explore the world with their favourite instrument: their mouth.

Provided that all accessible objects are safe (big enough that they can't be swallowed or inhaled and solid enough that no small part could break off), letting your baby put things in their mouth is fairly acceptable to most parents. Preventing this activity, towards which every baby is strongly and instinctively drawn, has the advantage of eliminating  extra sources of bacteria, but the disadvantage of limiting a behaviour which is the baby equivalent of browsing the Internet, consulting the dictionary or discovering a new novelist.

How can you turn your baby's natural instinct to 'mouth' things into a game? This is easy. Firstly, take the baby's mouthing as a sign of interest in something, as if they've asked you a question. You then follow up their interest by exploring the object with them, naming it and showing them its various properties – use all senses if you can. Can you look inside? Does it make a noise when you tap it? What does it smell like? Using all of the senses allows your baby to get the most out of their explorations.

Let's imagine your baby is desperately trying to lick your watch. You can take it off and show them what it is: the round part, the strap and buckle, the little holes on the strap, the hands of the quadrant, the colours, the noise it makes if you tap your fingers on it or if you place it close to your ear, how it looks on their wrist compared to yours, how your baby can fit it around their knee, how the hands can be moved around and so on. After all of your clever demonstrations your baby will still just want to lick it, but that's fine – you should never be disappointed when babies just want to do baby things, even when you showed them a hundred other possibilities!

Another 'game' that can be played involves channelling your baby's inclinations by providing safe toys that are particularly good to lick, suck, taste and otherwise explore. You can offer objects made of wood, rubber, plastic, metal and cloth, but also more organic items, such as a lemon, a cucumber or a potato. As well as being different from the materials that toys are made of, fruit and vegetables often have a more interesting smell and texture (provided they are clean, safe and no bits can come off and be swallowed or inhaled). In other words, rather than simply limiting your baby's independent explorations, you can redirect them in a way that is exciting for them as well as baby-proof.

Touching

I remember when my second daughter directed her hands decisively towards an object for the first time. She must have been less than three months old and, as I was pottering about in the kitchen, she resolutely dipped her hand into the jar of pesto I was holding, right up to her wrist. She would definitely have proceeded to lick it off if I hadn't stopped her. From then on, I vowed to pay more attention to her developing motor skills, but she caught me off guard on many more occasions.

Like mouthing, touching is a major exploratory activity, and one that is only apparently safer. Once the touching and grasping has been mastered, starting from about three months, the throwing begins. This bears a different set of risks altogether (including mental breakdowns in parents and siblings). Fortunately, in the first six months of life most babies are not able to move independently. This means that you can easily select the range of things that they are allowed to examine, scaling down the fun but also the risks. In fact, you can use the same strategy for touching as described for mouthing: offering your baby things that are safe as well as interesting to satisfy their hunger for new impressions.

Naming things

As an adult, you are aware that names are abstract – merely labels to help us easily refer to something. Babies, however, do not see it this way and as soon as they discover that there is a word for everything, they assume that each word belongs to one thing and that thing only. This is why small children get confused if you use the same name for different things (or indeed, different names for the same thing), such as saying 'milk' for the sweet, warm liquid that comes from your breast as well as for the cold, white drink that you get by opening the fridge.

Even when your child becomes a fluent speaker they will still treat names as if they are tangible, bound to the object they represent. It is difficult for a child to understand that names are only a convention and al fresco means the same as outside, just in another language and for no particular reason.

Because of the novelty of language, naming objects is a particularly interesting activity for a baby. You can play the naming game while you lounge in a waiting room or sit next to your baby in the car, simply by pronouncing the name of things that you offer or point out to your baby or that they independently reach out for: the orange blanket, the musical bear, Mummy's knee, etc. The most popular computer games for babies work in the very same fashion: the child presses a button/picture and the computer names that object.

Taking this game a step further, you can also christen toys and common objects: calling the teddy 'Ted', the blanket 'Blanky' and the bed 'Beddy' makes perfect sense to little ones, who regard animals, plants and inanimate objects as being endowed with human feelings and intentions. If baptising every article in your home and each plant in your garden proves too demanding, you can still name the objects around you in a way that makes them unique and eliminates confusion. 'Chair', for example, is too vague a concept, while referring to 'Daddy's chair', the 'baby chair', the 'squishy chair' and so on, gives more precise indications.

Having special names for your household's possessions makes communication easier: 'Let's sit on our raft' is much quicker and more effective than saying 'Let's sit on the brown stool by the window opposite the fireplace'. Don't worry if your list of names grows longer by the day – our long-term memory has unlimited capacity and we can never put too much strain on its resources. However, be aware that names that sound similar are more difficult to remember and may confuse both you and your baby.

Tip: Choosing names from different countries, such as Miguel, Monique or Mohammed, will foster an early aptitude for cultural understanding.

Anybody who has tried to learn a second language knows how exciting it is to feel that they are becoming able to understand and communicate in a way that was previously alien to them. Imagine travelling to a remote village in southern Italy, sitting in the local trattoria and placing a food order in your tentative Italian – when the waiter understands you, do you feel a sense of satisfaction (and not just because you are going to be fed)? The same will be true for your child as they develop their understanding of language.

As you guide your baby through the discovery of the many words that describe our world they will slowly build up knowledge and experience and overcome uncertainties and doubts. As you play with language together, you will also share the pleasure of each discovery, and if you can resist the temptation of putting a teaching hat on, the pleasure will be all the sweeter.

Talking

Talking to your baby can be very easy or very difficult, depending on the mood you are in. When you don't feel particularly communicative you can talk to yourself, keeping your little companion in mind as you give voice to passing thoughts or comment on the things you do. The simple chatter that your daily activities require can be enough to amuse your baby, and as newborns have a predisposition to learn language quickly and efficiently, anything to do with language feels novel and exciting.

Using a key phrase each time a certain situation occurs is the most simple 'game' you can play, and a very good way of making life more predictable for your newborn, who will soon decipher your message by associating the words you pronounce with what happens next. 'Bath time', 'Daddy's home', 'Mummy is taking you out', 'Let's read a book', etc. are all phrases that will soon be crystal clear to your baby if you take care to pronounce them emphatically just a few times. Your baby will also naturally interpret the sound, rhythm and intonation of your speech, together with your body language. Keeping sentences simple is always a good idea, using one- or two-word sentences to refer to things that your baby can see and touch. It is also helpful to use first names instead of pronouns as pronouns will be difficult for your baby to grasp: 'Mummy is here' rather than 'I am here'; 'Is Harry hungry?' rather than 'Are you hungry?' etc.

Speaking in 'Motherese' (the scientific name for baby-talk) is something most parents feel totally compelled to do, and for very good reason. As a species, we seem genetically predisposed to speak like nincompoops when we relate to babies (especially our own) and fortunately for us, they also have an innate preference for this communication style. For practical reasons it is best to use a combination of styles: Motherese and normally articulated everyday language – this will offer your baby a wider range of possibilities and significantly lowers the risk of losing your mind!

Talking on the phone

By 'talking on the phone' I don't mean the pretend conversations you may perform for your baby's sake with a fluorescent toy mobile. I mean the actual chatting you indulge in to keep in touch with friends and family. Watching you hold a lively conversation is far more entertaining than the majority of artificial pastimes you may purchase for your baby, and one that they never get tired of. Babies are naturally attracted to the sound of language and this makes it far too good an opportunity to waste.

Babies learn a great deal through imitation, without any need for encouragement and often without you being aware of them taking things in. What a baby discovers when they listen to you converse, gossip, inform, discuss, negotiate or simply speak, is that there is a lot you can do with words once you know a few of them.

My daughters never allowed me to peek at the computer screen or gaze at a magazine – not even for one minute – without throwing themselves in like furies, bashing, banging, ripping and attempting to get involved in other similarly disruptive ways. The mere sight of Mummy directing her attention to any written material was enough to trigger a disproportionate and excited determination to prevent it from happening. Even while breastfeeding, my second daughter would twist her neck round and wave her arms outwards if she heard the noise of pages being turned.

 On the contrary, both girls were quite happy to sit on my lap or next to me as I chatted away on the telephone. They would eavesdrop on my conversations as I comfortably sat back and kept a close eye on them while getting a few moments to myself. Seeing that they rather liked being exposed to my nattering, I didn't feel guilty for this time I took for myself. To me the most important thing was that they would not be brought up in silence or against the background noise of a television set (studies suggest the disturbance produced by a television which nobody is watching interferes with children's play).

Many babies protest at being excluded whenever their mum is engaged with someone or something other than them. If your baby gives you a hard time when you are having a conversation, you can involve them a little – looking at them, stroking them and handing them things while you talk will all help to make them feel included. Failing this, the speaker button will definitely pacify your baby, at least for a while, provided they are not too keen to join in the discussion.

As well as providing an interesting background for your baby's independent play, conversing on the phone is a remedy against the common feeling of isolation that many new mums feel. This notion is to be kept in mind, especially when the phone bill arrives and you need to remind yourself and/or the family's breadwinner that although cultivating a social network has its cost, its benefits are enormous.

Tip: Before getting started on a long-awaited phone call, check your baby's nappy and make sure they are not too close to becoming sleepy or hungry.

Excitement and anticipation

Anticipation games are all those activities where the fun is generated by an excited expectation of a predictable outcome. In this sense, 'peek-a-boo' is an anticipation game – the repetition of you appearing and disappearing allows your baby to predict that absence will be followed by presence. At the beginning, to see Mummy's face disappear is tinged with fear. After a few times, however, the fear is mixed with delight, for Mummy will soon reappear with a big smile, saying 'boo!' We play with anticipation as adults too; roller coasters, bungee jumping and skydiving all follow a similar logic: you know exactly what is going to happen, and you can tell beforehand that, at some point, you are going to be scared. However, being able to predict exactly what will happen turns fear into fun – a powerful feeling which in fact can become quite addictive.

Anticipation games
Incy Wincy spider climbed up the waterspout,
Down came the rain and washed the spider out,
Out came the sun and dried up all the rain,
So Incy Wincy spider climbed up the spout again

There is a reassuring message conveyed by this old nursery rhyme, which talks of changing fortunes, adversity, defeat and victory and where the spider's determination shines through. When you whisper or sing these words to your baby, 'walk' your fingers over their body, up and down, to mimic the heroic spider. The spout is, of course, on the baby's head, and the rain makes your fingers quickly run down to their tummy. When the rain is drying up your fingers can move in little circles before they 'climb up the spout again'. You can apply more or less pressure to vary the intensity of the tickling effect, as well as changing Incy Wincy's path. Compared to other tickling games, the excitement is milder but the fun is just as great.

You can imagine what happens from the baby's point of view when you play this game. Your hand starts tickling their foot or lower leg and then 'walks' up. When it is at about shoulder level it disappears to make itself felt on the neck and on the head. In the first three to four months the baby may fix on a point in front of them, smiling and concentrating on the sensations. Later on, the curiosity will emerge and they may put their hands on yours to feel your movements and figure out what is happening. They may also start following your hand with their eyes and, at some point, even push your hand onto their feet as a sign that they want you to start the game again. Unlike real tickling, the tickly sensations here are entirely predictable, making them feel completely safe and free to enjoy the game.

Here are a few equivalents to Incy Wincy Spider which you may remember from your own childhood:

Round and round the garden,
Like a teddy bear,
One step...
Two step...
Tickle you under there!

In Round and Round the Garden, you gently touch the palm of your baby's hand, moving your finger in circles. After marking the first two steps, you run your fingers up your baby's arms, tummy or sides, all the way up to the spot for tickling!

This little piggy went to market,
This little piggy stayed at home,
This little piggy had roast beef,
This little piggy had none,
And this little piggy cried 'wee, wee, wee!'
All the way home

This Little Piggy is a fun game to play as your baby becomes more aware of their fingers and toes, reciting each line of the rhyme and moving from finger to finger or toe to toe, giving it a little wiggle for extra effect. Some babies only enjoy this activity well after six months, possibly because they cannot hold their attention during the initial part of the game, when they are needed to wait as you move between fingers or toes. However, I have included it in this section as I have observed many other babies who do enjoy it, and smile with glee throughout the predictable sequence.

The element of surprise

One day, when you don't expect it, your baby will burst into laughter for the first time. It may happen after you've just sneezed, after you nearly tripped over or after you bumped your head on the corner of the kitchen cupboard. Having observed what makes babies laugh has led me to think that the common antics of slapstick comedy, such as slipping over stray banana skins, landing with your face in a creamy cake – as one commonly does – or being hit by a great bouncing object, are all situations that start having comic appeal in the first months of life.

The laughter provoked by both anticipation and surprise games is equivalent to a sigh of relief. While during anticipation games there is a gradual and slow build-up of tension towards an expected outcome, in the case of surprise the outcome is unexpected, and laughter erupts as a release of tension after a mild fright.

Babies are easily frightened, especially by noise and commotion. But what happens when they suddenly realise that the loud bang was just Mummy tripping over the kitchen mat and sending some pots flying? If the fright is not too intense your baby may enjoy a hearty laugh, wishing the show to be repeated. Many parents need no encouragement to play games involving excitement and surprise and take great pleasure in running around like mad things, simulating aeroplane flights and rolling around on the floor. Surprise, however, can also have a gentle nature – a sound, a tickle, an unexpected kiss on the nose.

Pulling faces

Pulling funny faces to entertain your baby is not as silly as it seems. The human face is the most appealing stimulus for babies – actions like blowing kisses, pursing your lips or clicking your tongue to make the noise of a galloping horse are all extremely interesting to them! In fact, it is far more likely that you will get tired of pulling faces and observing your baby's reaction before your baby grows tired of watching you. Even just looking is of interest to them – when you lovingly gaze at your baby from a close distance, you are offering them a form of entertainment that is both thrilling and pitched at the right stage of their development (no teenager, as you know, would endearingly smile while you look fondly into their eyes!) Older children and siblings are very good at this game and they often enhance it by producing a variety of sounds for the sake of their own entertainment, as well as the baby's. However, while these interactions are fun to watch, be prepared to abandon elegance and grace if you try to imitate them.

Pulling faces can be as simple as making a range of verbal sounds, wildly exaggerating the pronunciation to show your baby how you do it. An example would be pronouncing the word 'the' – a very definite display of putting your tongue between your teeth while making the appropriate sound. Another simple action they are likely to enjoy is if you shake your head as if saying no, while slowly getting closer to your baby

until the tips of your noses rub together (you may know it as 'Eskimo kissing'). It is surprising how long a baby's attention can be held by such simple, natural and cost-free means. You will know straight away when your baby has had enough, as they will start looking away – a sure sign that they need a little quiet time after all the excitement.

The psychology: Psychoanalyst René Spitz, famous for his observational studies of newborns, described how babies are genetically predisposed to respond to the basic eyes-nose-mouth configuration typical of the human face (as seen from the front, rather than the profile). He found that, starting from about the third month, all babies react with an endearing smile to seeing any face at the right distance. Following this discovery the 'smiling response' has been extensively studied, but researchers are still debating the exact nature of the newborn's smile, and whether we should see it as an automatic reflex or a social exchange.

Many experiments have tried to answer this question, for instance by showing masks and pictures of different types and proportions to babies. Interestingly, infants do smile even when presented with a mask, but only if it is realistic. When presented with two faces simultaneously, the babies spend more time gazing at the one that can be clearly classified as more attractive. Whatever the exact nature of the 'smiling response', it is highly significant that babies respond to seeing people in a special way from as early as 10 to 12 weeks of age.

Housekeeping games

Due to the loss of part of my rational brain during labour, I suffered from remarkable memory problems for many months after the birth of my children. As well as frequently getting lost mid-sentence, forgetting what I wanted to say, I never knew where anything was. Moving house during both pregnancies only made my short-term amnesia more apparent, for in a new home everything hides from you.

My favourite 'household game' therefore became looking for things. My daily search included all the items you can possibly need, from the address book, to the scissors or the telephone number I hastily scribbled on the corner of a newspaper. Thinking that my baby might wonder why her mother was always turning the home inside out, I made the best of a bad situation by playing the 'looking for things' game. From the moment I decided that the situation was so serious that it needed to be turned into a game, I must admit I actually had some fun inspecting the remote corners of the house, from behind the radiators to under the first layer of soil in the garden (you never know...).

There are clear advantages to playing this particular game. Firstly, since you need to spend time rummaging around, turning it into a playful show makes you feel like your time is not being completely wasted. Secondly, because young children believe that objects have feelings and intentions, the idea that something is purposely hiding from you and you have to discover its whereabouts is perfectly in line with a child's logic (and I wouldn't be surprised if there is some truth to this belief).

In the first six months of life most children cannot move about independently, and a lot of their time is spent looking around at their physical and human landscape. There are many activities you can involve them in by talking to them as you do things, and showing them what your actions are about. Babies love watching and listening and eventually imitating you. Dressing your daily chores with some explanation and playful performance can turn the uninspiring and menial activities that you cannot escape from into lively entertainment.

Singing

Singing is a wonderful activity for you and your baby to enjoy together, strengthening your bond even further. It can be uplifting, soothing or just plain fun! It is also beneficial for your baby in terms of language development as the words are often slowed down and more clearly pronounced. Don't worry if you are tone deaf and cannot carry a tune in a bucket – your baby is drawn to the sound of your voice and your singing will entertain and benefit them more than any perfectly executed recording.

Singing to calm your baby

'Johnny's So Long at the Fair' is an old song recounting worries about a boy who is taking a long time to come back home despite all the presents he promised to bring back. The refrain repeats somewhat light-heartedly: 'Oh dear, what can the matter be?' These words are perfectly suited to the unfortunately frequent times when babies become upset for causes which are often very difficult to establish (especially in the first six months).

During the first months of my daughter's life, between colic, teething and ordinary developmental frustration, I found myself quite often singing these words, hoping that somewhere I would find an answer. Each time I came up against one of my baby's bouts of frustration over something minor, such as not managing to reach a desired object, I had a mini dilemma: I couldn't take her too seriously, as I wanted to show her that the cause of her upset was insignificant; at the same time I did not want to ignore her, because, from her point of view, it was not. Livening up the situation with a song sometimes helped me to resolve this – it allowed me to acknowledge my baby's feelings without dwelling on them and helped me to distract her without running away from the issue, showing her that everything in life can be taken with a spoonful of sugar and a light heart.

> **Remember:** Every child has a right to have their business taken seriously, and no issue should be simply dismissed without at least a little consideration. Singing troubles away is not a way of teasing your baby or making fun of what they are going through – it is a cheerful acknowledgement of their woes.

What will happen in the baby's mind when instead of telling them something, you sing it to them? They will see how you pay attention to them without finding their troubles overwhelming, considering their predicament with loving concern but also with some detachment and humour. Babies can be very difficult and you may feel your patience is reaching its limit at times; however, you may find these limits can be extended when you sing, as by helping your child to take a step back, you help yourself to do the same.

Aside from calming your baby, singing can just be for entertainment's sake, especially when the words and music are accompanied by simple actions – normally clapping and waving your arms about. Knowing a few children's songs can be useful during long trips in the car, to entertain your baby together with an older sibling, or just to vary your play activities.

Here are just a few of the lovely songs perfect for singing on journeys:

Car Song (sung to The Farmer in the Dell)
We're riding in the car,
We're riding in the car,
Hi-ho, away we go!
We're riding in the car
We're riding, oh, so far,
We're riding, oh, so far,
Hi-ho, away we go!
We're riding, oh, so far.

Wheels on the Bus
The wheels on the bus go round and round,
Round and round; round and round
The wheels on the bus go round and round,
All day long.

You can add numerous verses to extend this one: 'The wipers on the bus go swish, swish, swish'; 'The horn on the bus goes beep, beep, beep'; 'The conductor on the bus says "Tickets please!"'; 'The doors on the bus they open and shut' – anything you can think of!

Choo-Choo Train
Here is the choo-choo train
Puffing down the track
Now it's going forward
Now it's going back
Now the bell is ringing
Now the whistle blows
What a lot of noise it makes
Everywhere it goes!

Singing to help your child fall asleep

Singing is a lovely way to help your baby prepare for sleep. It is easily built into a night-time routine and can form part of that all-important calming ritual that relaxes your baby into slumber. Singing to your baby as you watch them fall asleep can be a beautiful and rewarding experience, providing you with some of your fondest memories. Remember, the opportunities for such intimate exchanges will be limited – one day a 'No Entry' sign will appear on your teenager's bedroom door.

Rock-a-bye Baby

Rock-a-bye baby, on the tree top
When the wind blows, the cradle will rock
When the bough breaks, the cradle will fall
And down will come baby, cradle and all.

Cradle Song

Golden slumbers kiss your eyes
Smiles await you when you rise
Sleep pretty baby, do not cry
And I will sing a lullaby.

Cares you know not, therefore sleep
While over you, a watch I'll keep
Sleep pretty darling, do not cry
And I will sing a lullaby.

Are You Sleeping? (Frère Jacques)

Are you sleeping, are you sleeping?
Brother John, Brother John?
Morning bells are ringing, morning bells are ringing
Ding ding dong, ding ding dong.

It is true that your baby will wake up during the night, they will call for you, and your rest will be disrupted. This is why some parents opt for the popular method whereby you teach your child to fall asleep by themselves from day one by remaining impervious to their screams and protests when you put them down in their bed and walk out. Like many of my colleagues, I am in disagreement with this drastic approach, and the reported evidence of its success is rather overstated. Many parents are embarrassed when this strategy fails, despite them withstanding nights of tears, rage and desperation – therefore they often keep quiet about its failure. In spite of claims to the contrary, teaching a child to sleep by themselves is not necessarily an easy task and it can seldom be done in a definite time frame. It requires time and effort and, with the exception of a few lucky cases, there will be ups and downs in your child's ability to manage whole nights by themselves.

It is perfectly normal and predictable that your baby will take some time before they manage to sleep through the night – even if some enviable (or boastful) parent tells you how they never lost an hour of sleep, this simply may not be the case for you. I certainly lost more than a few hours' sleep but I don't regret it a bit.

How to handle the tricky issue of sleep is far beyond the scope of this book, but I will say that it is important that you choose the system which is best suited to your own personality, needs, resources and family structure. Do not feel under pressure to follow a parenting trend or to heed advice you did not ask for. As sleep specialist Theresa Shumard puts it: 'Parents should be careful about using someone else's method to get their baby to sleep. Consideration of any advice should be approached with sensitivity to the infant's temperament and individual family situations.'

Be aware: A cultural and, at times, ideological component is always present in matters concerning child-rearing practices, including statements like 'Children must learn to fall asleep on their own.' This is a particularly Western viewpoint, where it is customary for each child to have their own room and sleep separately from their parents and siblings. Western culture also tends to value independence more than interconnectedness. Therefore, whatever you do, be aware that there is a variety of ways to resolve parenting problems, each with its own advantages and disadvantages and each being more suited or less suited to your own predicament.

Music and dancing

Your baby may not walk or talk yet but they will probably enjoy dancing with you. Babies take to music and dancing very early on but at this stage 'dancing' with your baby will just mean a gentle swing that barely follows the rhythm of some music playing in the background. Later on, as soon as they are able to stand and take their first steps, they can rock their body and shake their heads as the music starts. As well as gently swinging your baby to the sound of the music, you can follow the rhythm by patting them, walking your fingers over them, or marking the tempo in any other way.

Listening to music of any type is going to help you manage tasks, as well as providing you with stimulating company. It was thanks to my children that I discovered classical music, when I was looking for an effective diversion from grey and miserable days. From the Carnival of the Animals, to Peter and the Wolf or the Nutcracker, there are many different examples of classical tunes perfectly suited to non-verbal conversations with babies, toddlers and children. Babies have no preconceptions about which music is for dancing and which is for listening to, so you should not be surprised if a Mozart concerto for violin stimulates frantic hand flapping!

Remember: When you sing and dance with your baby, you do much more than that – you create intimacy, you let musical creativity into your day and you make your feelings known by sharing a moment of joy, boredom, melancholy or excitement.

Reading the first books

I am one of those people who cannot finish a book unless they like it, and the same goes for baby literature: to read a book to my children, I have to find something appealing, interesting or amusing in it, or the boredom becomes a torment. However, when I find the right story, reading can feel life-changing – it comforts, entertains and stimulates me; it brings me closer to other people and situations and gives me stories to think about other than my own personal ones.

To choose the best books for your baby you only need to pick something from the vast array of literature for babies that you genuinely like and enjoy. You may feel inspired by the images, characters, names, situations or atmospheres that are brought to life; you may like the quality of the materials, the style of the pictures or the shades of colour; you may appreciate the story, the drawings or the combination of both. Whatever your preferences, you will naturally ignite your baby's interest just by delving into something that pleases you.

Children depend on your interpretation of written words and images to enjoy books, and it is through such interpretation that they get their first taste of literature. When you point to various details in the pictures, marvel at the colours or demonstrate what can be done with the tactile and sensory parts of the book, you effectively show them how to contemplate, explore and discover – things that propel you beyond your first impressions to a deeper understanding and appreciation of things. As your baby grows older you will be able to tell more complex and articulate stories, and as you turn the pages to read something simple, you will naturally punctuate it with exclamations, whispers and suchlike. You will also discover how your poetic fantasy and willingness to invent things is still alive and well when you can construe an adventurous tale with only a carrot, the sun, a snail, and a boy wearing a blue hat!

Key points

- Ordinary, everyday care has the most impact on your child's future development – not exceptional, rare events.

- Preconceived ideas and expectations can often be counter-productive – nothing is as relevant and important as your own observations in determining what will work for your baby.

- Everything your baby does has a meaning and a purpose. Believe that there is something to be seen and that it is worth seeing.

- Observation is important – it helps you to learn about your baby and for them to learn about you. You cannot know everything right away so don't be afraid to take all the time you need to get to know each other.

- We are not used to looking at our surroundings as if we had never seen them before. This is why your baby will be interested in many things you might not expect.

- Offer your baby safe and interesting things to mouth or touch, rather than restricting their explorations.

- Use a key phrase each time a certain situation occurs – this makes life more predictable for your newborn and will allow them to start understanding language.

- Involve your baby in everyday tasks, whether it's washing up, preparing the lunch or talking on the phone.

- Singing troubles away is a cheerful way to acknowledge your baby's woes.

- Choose methods which are best suited to your own personality, needs, resources and family structure. Do not feel under pressure to follow parenting trends or to follow unrequested advice.

- When you sing and dance with your baby you create intimacy, you let musical creativity into your day and you make your feelings known by sharing a moment of joy, boredom, melancholy or excitement.

- Choose baby books you like – your enthusiasm and pleasure will naturally spark your baby's interest.

Chapter 3

6 to 12 Months

So, you have now managed to adapt to the slower pace of life that comes with a newborn, accepted that life isn't just about doing things and you have mastered a degree of boredom and 'stillness'. Well, that is about to change! The challenges and rewards of this period are dramatically different to the first six months; they also require a different set of skills, physical resources, personality and outlook on life. Some parents much prefer this type of challenge to that of the early days of babyhood, when you thought you were living in a French movie – always waiting for something to happen. Whatever your viewpoint, you will experience these months as a major shift, either with a sigh of relief or with the feeling that you have a new mountain to climb.

As your baby matures you have to deal with two major issues:

1. Their increased mobility with its related drive towards independence. This is not just about crawling and walking! Ever more frequently, and with increasing urgency, you need to watch out that they do not topple over from their newly acquired sitting position or put small things in their mouth, as well as ensuring they do not crawl to dangerous objects or spots, and eventually, that they do not walk or run into danger.

2. The unavoidable bursts of frustration caused by the gap between their ambitions and their abilities. It is a hard-wired instinct that pushes your baby forward all the time, making them want to touch that soft toy, grab that ball or master a new sound – no amount of naturally occurring frustration will make the baby give up on their curiosity and daily practice of new skills (although unfortunately, the frustrations imposed by an overly strict upbringing do have an impact on a child's keenness to explore). Reaching developmental milestones is very hard work and behind every little, seemingly ordinary achievement there is tireless commitment and effort.

When you play with a child at this developmental stage it is useful to keep in mind that their efforts will eventually be repaid, independently of what you do. This will help you not to panic when you see your baby getting stuck, which then helps you resist the temptation to rush their natural progress. A supportive and loving presence at the baby's side is all that is required – you do not need to make everything easy or go the opposite way to give them extra challenges. At this stage your baby does not need motivational training or rewards – it is not your praise or assistance they are seeking but the conquest of new territories!

This stage of development involves facing new issues and tackling problems which did not necessarily emerge in the first six months. Differences in parenting styles and attitudes towards your child's behaviour become increasingly more apparent in this period and it is a good thing to be aware of your stance on things. Such viewpoints are often influenced by your personal preferences, culture, personality or past experiences. However, except for extreme parenting styles (mostly originating from under or over involvement), there is no right or wrong way to approach your baby's first steps towards independence. What is important is asking yourself certain questions so you understand and feel comfortable in your own position: How much will you allow your baby to explore on their own? How close or far back will you feel able to stand? How will you regard their first experiments involving messiness and dirt? How big a risk will you allow them to take for the sake of their learning? Asking these questions is more important than trying to find the right answers.

Tip: It can be very useful to watch other parents tackle the same issues in different ways. Once again (I cannot stress this enough) it is important not to measure your baby and yourself against them, but to simply observe others in order to reflect on the range of possibilities that exist when it comes to taking a stance with your baby. We often do something not because we choose that specific course of action but because we regard it as the only way forward – this is why it is so beneficial to reflect on the reasons underlying our behaviour. When you ask yourself 'Why am I doing X and not Y?' you become aware, just through genuinely pondering the question, that there are many more options open to you.

Understanding what your baby wants

Trying to work out what your baby wants (although you don't have to necessarily give it to them) is extremely important. When they were two months old it was much easier – they were usually either hungry, sleepy or in pain. However, as they grow up and actively start looking for new ways to satisfy their curiosity, the reason behind tears and tantrums becomes more difficult to guess. If your baby is unsettled you may try to understand their point of view by verbalising feelings, as mentioned in the second chapter. For example, you may say: 'Oh! Mia looks unhappy. Let's see. You had your rest and your dinner and your nappy is clean. What could the matter be?' You then formulate other reasons that might apply to Mia and without any obvious cause for her distress you try to make her feel better by comforting her and/or offering distraction in the form of play. Some of your strategies will not have any positive effect, while others will sooner or later work. In such an easy way, and just by being mindful, you do three important things:

1. You take your baby seriously even if you are not sure of the nature of their upset. When a child knows that they are being heard and attended to, they build a general confidence in their ability to find comfort from others (something which is linked to self-esteem). It does not matter whether you give them what they want or not. You may have very good reasons to refuse them your shiny brand new mobile phone, but it helps if you let them know that you understand the bad luck of being little and desperately wanting what you can't have.

2. You prevent them from seeking strategies to get your attention by other less civilised means. As mentioned in the first chapter, all children are attention-needing, not just attention-seeking; if you give attention when your child initially requests it, whether you go along with their wishes or not, there are real advantages for you both.

3. You get to know your baby, learning about their own tastes and inclinations through trial and error. They remain free to be their own person and do not need to conform to your expectations: you are genuinely trying to understand their point of view.

As a new mum, I felt a cold terror each time my first baby was desperately unhappy and I couldn't figure out how to help her, especially if I was in a public place. As parents, we may feel helpless and inadequate even when we can see that we have not done anything wrong. In these cases it is not important to guess the real reason behind your child's tears but to test a few hypotheses and look for what might help. A simple example may clarify this point. Let's say you are sitting on a park bench on the first sunny day of summer with your seven-month-old and, just as you lay back and relax, they start whinging and whining. You change their position on your lap but this makes them worse. You give them a toy and they push it away, stepping up the volume of complaint. You wonder whether they are hot and remove their shoes and socks to see if this makes them better. Your baby then catches a glimpse of their toes and is fascinated by them in the sunlight! They start playing with them, bringing them to their mouth and desperately trying to explore these wiggly things at the end of their feet. Even if they were not actually hot, you have diverted them and captured their attention. What I call 'emergency play' will often come out of this type of situation, adding to your personal repertoire of games and problem-solving skills, as well as getting to know what works for your baby.

Do not underestimate the power of involvement in pacifying your baby! Babies often need attention at the most inconvenient times, fretting and whining unbearably while you, let's say, are trying to put dinner together. A seemingly minor issue like this can be rather stressful, especially if it is repeated over many days, leading you to dread cooking more than you ever did. In this case, and in many similar instances, the problem arises from your baby's desire to be involved at counter level. For them, being on the floor is like watching a film with 60 per cent of the screen blocked and this cooking business is far too interesting not to see everything! At this stage of development your baby's physical growth is surpassed by a monstrous surge of curiosity but you can reduce their demanding interferences by allowing them a full view of what is going on. Whether you sit down and potter at their level or scoop them up so that they can be part of the action, this kind of 'play' is what your baby will love most. These everyday activities are new to your baby and endless fun can be generated by affording them simple pleasures: throwing potatoes as you peel them, ripping teabags open as you take them

out of the tin, pulling clothes out of your wardrobe and tugging socks out of their drawers. All of this can have the feeling of 'forbidden fun': something permitted under exceptional (though maybe not infrequent) circumstances, in exchange for a moment of peace or as an emergency measure in the face of unbearable protests.

In many instances the cause of your baby's upset can remain unclear despite many educated guesses, and this can be tricky if you are among those who like to be in control and find clear and precise answers. To overcome a sense of not getting it right (which at this stage of your baby's development is unavoidable) you must keep in mind that what is important here is the process of asking – your own open and tolerant curiosity about your baby will lead you to learn about their personality; something which will emerge out of the many contradictory impressions that you gather along the way.

Making choices for your child

When shopping, do you find yourself overwhelmed by the vast array of different baby toys and books, wondering what would be best for your baby? You may be considering how 'useful' any given item will be in terms of its educational value, its power to keep your baby entertained, and its (hopefully minimal) impact on mess and noise levels. However, such items can only be useful if your baby actually engages with them! What is truly useful is a toy or book that your baby really enjoys – this will be what they dedicate their attention to for longer periods of time, learning and developing through their play. You may end up with an exceptionally messy, noisy or sticky play area, but letting your baby's inclinations direct your choices has a definite positive side.

So how do you go about choosing something they will enjoy? Well, in the first six months it was ideal to choose what you liked best among the many age-appropriate options in order to communicate real interest and enjoyment to your newborn, who could not indicate their budding tastes. At this stage, however, it is possible to test their reactions and see if they are more or less interested in particular topics, sizes, shapes, colours, materials, etc. For example, when choosing a 'buggy friend' (those books that you can attach to the buggy), you can hand them a few different ones to see which they are most attracted to. The choice they make will hardly be random and, as long as you don't choose something you really detest, no harm can come from letting them decide!

Another obvious source of guidance to help you choose a toy or an activity is what 'the experts' say. There is certainly nothing wrong with trying out what is suggested by those who should know what is best for your baby, provided you keep in mind that current fashion, culture and values do influence the type of advice each generation of parents will receive. If you can pick up suggestions from reliable sources and adapt them to your baby without becoming too fanatical about them, your skills will certainly be enhanced. It is also a good idea to listen to more than one point of view before making up your own mind.

FYI: In terms of books, new research claims that children understand photographs better than drawings, as photographs are more similar to what they represent. Many publishing houses have taken this on board and produce books for babies and toddlers which have very colourful pictures but not a single drawing in them.

An important thing to remember when choosing on behalf of your baby is that, at this stage, they are still attracted to the small details of objects and may often fail to appreciate the whole. You may find, for example,

that your baby loves an expensive soft toy, but when you look more carefully it is actually the label they are fascinated by. The same goes for books: they might hand you a book to read because they are after that particular noise you make as you try to impersonate the crab on page two; similarly, they might be fond of that light-up musical cow just because they like the feel of its tail, and so on. You must not think that your baby doesn't really appreciate something just because they focus on what may seem like an insignificant detail to you. Discouraging babies from doing what we regard as 'meaningless' is like rushing them to grow up and become sensible, average and predictable; the more similar to us the better. Unfortunately, conformity to the behaviour of the majority is an extremely powerful instinct – one which there is no need to reinforce. The only thing that matters is to provide age-appropriate stimulation that entertains and fascinates your baby, whether it makes sense to you or not. Valuing your child's tastes and inclinations, no matter how outlandish, may teach them the value and beauty of becoming their own person.

Give your baby confidence

In the second semester you will have a chance to learn a great deal more about your child's personality. According to child psychiatrists Stella Chess and Alexander Thomas, the attitude towards new situations and challenges, particularly how prone a baby is to giving up or persevering, is one of the basic traits that a baby is born with. However, regardless of your baby's innate tenacity and tolerance of frustration, it is important to praise their attempts at exploring, trying out new things, tackling obstacles and so on.

As family therapist Miriam Chachamu points out, praise must not be an evaluation, but more like an approving and enthusiastic description of why we think our baby is doing well. Something like: 'Look at you! You can stand holding yourself with just one hand!' is much better than, 'What a good boy!' By being descriptive, highlighting the details of our children's feats, we avoid judgement (though a positive one) and we give them much more information about why we approve.

On the other hand, when your baby is unsuccessful they will learn this lesson by themselves – telling them things like 'It was too difficult for you', 'You can't do it' or 'Wait until you're older' will only add insult to injury.

Remember: we all share a natural fear of going wrong and we all make mistakes in the process of learning. It is important to develop a degree of confidence and boldness and a willingness to take risks for the sake of our own happiness.

Playing like a baby is about spending time together where neither you nor your baby feel there is anything to prove or anybody to please. If you protect this time and shelter it from our society's obsession with optimum performance you will give your baby a wonderful gift, allowing them to try out their developing skills in a more natural way. It is paramount that while you play with your baby you stop in your tracks whenever you find yourself expressing judgements about their skills, however excellent or poor they are.

I recently witnessed the effects of a judgemental 'do it only if you are good at it' upbringing when playing with my daughter in my GP's waiting room. Some leaves had fallen off a plant and I was showing my daughter how she could blow a leaf to lift it up in the air when a four-year-old boy approached us looking shy but rather interested. I found a suitable leaf for him and told him to have a go. He said he would like to but he wasn't sure whether he would be able to blow it up in the air. After some encouragement he finally tried it and rather liked it! When he walked away half an hour later he was clutching his leaf tightly, possibly to continue the game elsewhere, or as a trophy of his success. I was left wondering whether it can be right that a four-year-old should have such fear of failure like this little boy had. How do children learn that one must be good at things? Why doesn't everybody show them that, at least when you play, anything goes?

Setting boundaries for exploration

In order to put reasonable and fair limits on your baby's explorations you must first decide what you are going to allow and what you are going to ban. You can keep quite a few things outside the reach of your baby, but you can't ask them to play with their toys only. The decision about what can be permitted is mostly personal and varies a lot across cultures but the following criteria can help you decide. If, even after baby-proofing your home, you are constantly saying 'No!', you are probably setting too many restrictions. However, if you have no time to do anything because you are constantly running around after your baby to clear up their mess, you might need to be a bit stricter and limit their exploratory activities.

It is better to set a few strong rules in those areas that one regards as most important, rather than trying to limit a wide range of things. It helps you to be determined and firm, it prevents you from feeling guilty about saying no and it helps the child to understand that when you say no you really mean it. Safety is the paramount issue – as long your baby's explorations are safe, the messy, noisy and highly inconvenient explorations are all tools of development. Limiting them is necessary; forbidding them is not.

Before you start setting the boundaries try to allow a bit of experimentation, even if this means cleaning up a lot of mess and picking up broken bits. Before you say 'Enough now', you can take the opportunity to understand what is happening from your baby's point of view, sharing their surprise, dismay or fun at observing natural phenomena. It is also useful to help your baby fully appreciate the consequences of their actions before you start cleaning up any mess. How is your baby meant to know that they have done something 'wrong'? If you seethe in silence while cleaning up, how are they meant to know that you aren't just joining in their clever game? They may be confused by your silence and want to try their trick again straight away to see if you are a bit more appreciative second time around! By the same token, if you scream and shout as if your football team had just scored an own goal, how are they meant to understand that it's because of what they have done?

Let's say your child has just turned their bowl of soup upside down. A way to tackle this issue is to describe what has happened, and explain in plain English that it is not a good thing. For example: 'See? Your food is all over the table now! There is no food left on the plate, and baby is hungry! What are we going to eat now?' Then the second time you go to feed your baby, you calmly prevent them from playing with their dinner. With time and consistency they will naturally internalise a general rule about not playing with food at the dinner table, although at times, and depending on their temperament, they might want to 'test the boundaries' by trying this trick once or twice more.

Cause and effect

As the first birthday approaches, spatial awareness becomes more accurate and your baby will actively try to see what is behind, beneath and inside things – this reflects their development in understanding cause and effect. As with all newly emerging skills, this awareness creates new opportunities for play, but this time your baby can be the director of their own entertainment. Initially, you had to demonstrate how a ball would disappear if you rolled it under the couch and how you could find it again (together with a six-month dust deposit) by looking underneath it. Now they can start putting this new knowledge into practice, whether it's tipping over the milk bottle in order to observe the liquid forming white puddles, slapping the surface of the bath water in order to feel it splash, or throwing things across the room.

These cause and effect games are your baby's version of scientific experiments. They happily perform them on the world around them, and their first one is likely to be 'Dropping Objects on the Floor While Sitting in a High Chair'. Honestly, this experiment is not to test the limits of your patience! Some experiments are directed at humans rather than objects, but this is not all about 'testing the boundaries' (an overused concept

which is much more useful to understand the terrible twos and beyond). In the period that goes from six to twelve months, babies learn rapidly that crying, laughing, smiling, coughing, throwing, etc. all have powerful effects on the people around them. Babies register these reactions in a non-verbal, instinctive way and they soon know exactly what to expect. I have seen an eight-month-old purposely coughing and spluttering and then laughing as soon as the expression of terror appeared in their anxious mother's eyes!

But what exactly does it mean to conduct an experiment? Experiments are actions performed under controlled conditions, to prove that a relationship of cause and effect exists between two things. For example, you might be interested to find out whether increasing vitamin E intake through eating more fresh green vegetables causes your skin to look healthier. To prove it, you must exclude other factors which muddy the waters, influencing what you are observing. For example: is your skin looking healthier because you are eating more green vegetables or because in order to increase the intake of vegetables you are consuming fewer chips? You must also be able to say with confidence that the results of your carefully planned experiment are not due to chance. Now, let's say you manage to prove that more green vegetables means healthier-looking skin – you still have not answered why. Why is your skin now looking healthier? Was the change caused by increasing your vitamin E intake or was it something else, like eating more fibre? Would any other green vegetable have had a similar effect? To understand the causes and how it all happens, a whole new set of experiments needs to be carried out, with no close end in sight.

My discussion about the advantages and pitfalls of experimental research leads to this point: your baby is a far superior scientist compared to the average professional researcher. First of all, your baby has the advantage of blind and reckless determination, which leads them to explore and experiment all day long, with few breaks, no remuneration and little fear of the risks involved. Because of the need for safety precautions, most babies are limited in the amount they can test and experiment with. However, as long as these precautions are in place, be as liberal as you want! Let them rip pages of books designated for the purpose, let them taste CDs, plant soil – they will nevertheless push the limits to what they can possibly be allowed to try. Through this attitude and behaviour babies make sure that they don't leave anything to chance. Furthermore, when an interesting effect is obtained – and pretty much everything holds an interest at this stage – babies don't just try it once or twice. To do these things only once is never enough, as babies, just like scientists, want to be sure of their findings by replicating their experiments to see if their findings are the same over time and across different situations.

Has your baby started pushing things along? Compared to the previous examples, pushing something around for fun, such as a toy car, is definitely an advanced skill. It requires motor dexterity (good hand movements), coordination and control, and a new awareness of the outcome of a complex sequence of actions. As the famous paediatrician T. Berry Brazelton points out, in the first year of life it is not uncommon for a child to turn a toy car upside down to try and figure out the mechanics of its movements. Similarly, as your baby begins to understand the movement of rolling, you will find that they have a great deal of interest in following the rolling objects all around the house. Crouching to check how far they go, and in which direction, becomes quite amusing for them!

Mirrors are another great discovery during this period. The famous 'Rouge Test' – where lipstick is put on the baby's nose and they are put in front of a mirror to see at what age they start touching their own nose rather than the nose in the reflection – demonstrated it is only at around 15 months that children start to grasp the concept of seeing a reflection of themselves. However, the interest in these objects starts much earlier on, and you can find plenty of baby books with plastic mirrors in them which are safe to play with. Mirrors also offer interesting variations on peek-a-boo games: you and your baby can repeatedly walk in front of a mirror and then suddenly step away from it, making your reflections disappear as quickly as they appeared.

Finally, a fun cause and effect game that becomes attractive towards the end of your baby's first year is construction. They may like to watch you piling up bricks into a tower and then knocking them over, or they may clumsily put a few blocks together themselves. Whatever their actions, they are experimenting with gravity, trying out numerous objects and tricks to see if they can defy its laws!

Presence and absence

Presence and absence is something that can form the basis for a lot of fun. Haven't we all enjoyed, at least once, watching an illusionist make something disappear up his sleeve and reappear in his hat? A lot of entertainment is based on special effects and visual illusions and it should not be surprising that the foundations of this interest are laid in our infancy. The special effects that impress babies are low-cost (free, in fact) and easy to produce: all you need is time to play!

The most common example of a presence and absence game is peek-a-boo, where hiding one's face, or just one's eyes (absence) is followed by their sudden reappearance (presence). This game's popularity with children hasn't decreased over generations and more or less identical versions exist across all cultures. There is a good reason for this: very young children think that they can hide from you just by covering their eyes. With this logic, peek-a-boo becomes a much more interesting and exciting experience, similar to playing hide and seek.

The psychology: In a recent experiment, researchers from St Andrew's University asked children between two and four to say whether a partially covered Teletubby could be seen by a teddy bear which was sitting opposite them. When the Teletubby was completely hidden or when only his face could be seen and his body was blocked from view the children got it right. However, when the Teletubby's whole body was visible but the face was covered, the children wrongly assumed that it was out of sight. Interestingly, the children didn't make mistakes when they had to judge whether a regular object could be seen, even if it was partially covered from view. If any part of the object was visible, then they considered it visible. Therefore, the eyes and the face must hold a particular value when it comes to being visible or invisible. With this in mind, it is no wonder that eye contact has such a powerful effect on babies.

Another reason for the popularity of this type of game is that at around eight to nine months of age, babies acquire what is known as 'object permanence'. This means that they learn to look for an object after it has been hidden – they now realise that things continue to exist even outside their range of vision. Before this milestone has been reached, babies will not look for something once it is hidden from view, even if you have slowly moved an object of interest behind your back, in front of their very eyes. As T. Berry Brazelton suggests in his book, *Touchpoints: Birth to Three*, playing games involving presence and absence can help children practise their newly learnt awareness and reinforce their new knowledge that someone or something 'gone' will soon be found again.

The psychology: A famous description of a presence and absence game was made by Freud in 1920. At that time Freud was staying with his extended family, and he took the opportunity to observe the activities of his grandson over a few days. This is how he describes what has since been known as the 'wooden reel game':

This good little boy had an occasional disturbing habit of taking any small objects he could get hold of and throwing them away from him into a corner, under the bed, and so on, so that hunting for his toys and picking them up was often quite a business. As he did this he gave vent to a loud, long-drawn-out 'o-o-o-o', accompanied by an expression of interest and satisfaction. His mother and the writer of the present account agreed in thinking that this was not a mere interjection but represented the German word 'fort' ['gone']. I eventually realized that it was a game and that the only use he made of any of his toys was to play 'gone' with them. One day I made an observation which confirmed my view. The child had a wooden reel with a piece of string tied round it. It never occurred to him to pull it along the floor behind him, for instance, and play at its being a carriage. What he did was to hold the reel by the string and very skilfully throw it over the edge of his curtained cot so that it disappeared into it, at the same time uttering his expressive 'o-o-o-o'. He then pulled the reel out of the cot again by the string and hailed its reappearance with a joyful 'da' ['there']. This, then, was the complete game of disappearance and return.

(Beyond the Pleasure Principle)

Children appear to prefer the second phase of presence and absence games, when the object is found, rather than the first, more theatrical one, when they seem to want to get rid of it. Freud's description of the 'wooden reel game' captures a feature of the peek-a-boo game which develops around the end of the first year: when your child wants to take

control of the appearance and disappearance, as well as watching you do it. It is likely they will practise it themselves by covering their eyes and making the world disappear, before uncovering them and getting it all back. From this point on, you can also expect to be called with great urgency, only to discover that your baby wants you to find them while they expectantly hide from you underneath a tea towel.

As with most of these games, it is more likely that you will lose interest in this activity before your baby does. Repetition is not boring at this age, and parents are still on their own in their quest for variation and change!

Imitation

A vast amount of what your baby learns is acquired through imitation. Through imitation, our brain rehearses any action we see others perform, allowing us to learn quickly and efficiently just through watching. However, each new skill you observe in your baby has been in the making for quite some time; that wave goodbye/new word/pincer grasp is the product of several weeks of dedicated practice as your baby quietly rehearses the complex action. During this time your baby is continuing to mature both physically and mentally and this cornerstone of development will give you a powerful new tool for interaction and play.

You can see the first signs of imitation as early as the first three months of life. At this time, it is a slightly different form of imitation: more primitive, instinctive and almost involuntary. It is described by psychologists as 'mirroring'; a concept introduced by the British paediatrician and psychoanalyst Donald Winnicott to describe the interactions between mothers and babies. The mirroring theory is this: every baby can see an image of themselves in their mother's eyes, where they can also read an elaborated version of their own feelings; feelings which are still unknown to them. It is as if you had never seen your own figure before and someone else helped you to imagine yourself by providing you with a description. Through your own interactions with your baby, you interpret their state of mind and reflect it back to them, with all the feelings, emotions or moods that they have consciously or unconsciously picked up. Your baby, in turn, starts recognising some of their feelings as they see them reflected in your eyes and demeanour.

The psychology: Less than twenty years ago, researchers working at the Italian University of Parma discovered why we are able to imitate and feel what others feel. They found that when we watch someone else perform an action a sub-set of neurons, our mirror neurons, act as if it was us performing that action and not someone else. The amazing fact is that the same neurons are activated when we perform an action as when we simply witness it. They provide the basis for empathy, suggesting that there is a deeper physical connection between people than we previously thought.

As your baby's imitation skills improve and become more noticeable, you will find they start using gestures to communicate: pointing, copying your signs for hurrah! (hands up), clapping, waving goodbye, blowing a kiss, hissing for 'hot', and raising their hands in a half circle above their head for 'big'. At this stage it can be fun to play simple games like making interesting noises or performing actions like banging a drum, blowing or clapping and waiting for your baby to try and do the same. However, don't feel you have to limit imitation to encouraging your baby to mimic you – it can be great fun (for both of you) if you try to ape what your baby does too. Your baby will soon realise what is happening and after their initial surprise they may continue the interaction or try new tricks to see if you are still following them. As well as with gestures, it can also be fun to mimic some of your baby's 'games'. The simplest activities – moving an object from left to right, loading a truck with bits and bobs and then unloading it, giving something out and then taking it back – are often games that you would not normally consider without your baby's suggestion.

Be aware: It is useful to keep in mind that babies and toddlers do not only observe and imitate when we ask them to, but are like powerful video recorders: switched on most of the time and able to store an unlimited amount of material. One day you will be shown a shockingly accurate replay of your own accent, phrases, attitudes and gestures! The obvious downside of imitation is that it applies equally to good and bad things – your child will not be selective in imitating virtuous acts over less desirable ones. Verbal and physical aggression, for example, are very quickly picked up when witnessed in others – this is also true for adults, especially if those we observe are of a similar age, gender and culture to us.

Games involving imitation are often also about role playing – when your baby wants to wear your glasses, put on your shoes, or use your mobile, they are copying you. They want to be like you. Imitation is about building bridges across people, empathising, swapping places – sharing your inner world with someone else and having them share their inner world with you.

Chasing

On average, babies start crawling at around eight months and walking towards the end of their first year. Dashing about, with or without a goal in mind, then becomes a new and exciting type of play for them. This activity will hold its appeal in different forms throughout your child's life, in some cases continuing well into adulthood. In fact, as adults we take chasing very seriously – spectacular chases are a trademark of any good Hollywood blockbuster and well-paid and highly respectable sports consist in nothing other than chasing something. However, the less sophisticated version I'm discussing here becomes highly attractive at around nine months of age.

Because of your baby's enthusiasm to move about independently, their uncoordinated and overstated movements as they run for their life can make the chase quite amusing. In some cases the beginning of the game can be signalled by a special 'I-am-about-to catch-you' look and posture; in others the actual words will have an effect. However, crawling after a baby is incredibly physically challenging and, unless your home has a soft carpet, quite painful too! Babies can crawl at a reasonable speed and with some ease because they have different body proportions to ours. As they grow it is their head which reaches adult proportions first, followed by their torso and finally their arms and legs. So, if after crawling a few metres you cannot bear it any longer, it is not because you are terribly unfit – you are not as good as your baby at moving on all fours because nature has meant it to be that way.

> **The psychology:** It seems that these baby proportions, which are present in many other species (think of the big heads of puppies and kittens), are the reason why we find babies 'cute'. It is believed that these features are intended to protect the young from adult aggression.

Chasing has all the ingredients of a good game: suspense, excitement, exercise, the need for quick action and decision-making, physical exploration, playful competition, negligible risk (especially if the baby is still crawling; otherwise safety precautions must be taken) and a happy ending. As well as motor skills, chasing requires social and emotional abilities. This becomes apparent when you suddenly stop and let your baby guess what your next move is going to be. At this point your baby will try to read your expression and body language and will often successfully gauge where you are heading next. Chasing then becomes a game of reading each other's intentions – something babies learn to do accurately early on (apparently by the first six months). Throughout the chase your baby will also be aware that your only motive for running after them is play – nothing else.

Playing in small spaces

When I was due to have my first child I didn't understand why I wasn't supposed to put her straight into the little Moses basket I had bought for her, especially since finding one for our tiny bedroom had been such an ordeal. It was then that I heard for the first time that newborns need a tightly fitted space around them in order to feel comfortable and safe.

Keeping this very simple fact in mind will prove useful in varying the usual games you play with your baby. I found, for example, that when my baby climbed into a small shallow basket, more or less the size of a hat box but not as deep, she was entertained for quite some time, and helped her to concentrate on other activities as well. Of course, when babies realise that they can be pushed around in the basket as though it were a miniature trailer, the game becomes even more entertaining for them (although more tiresome and demanding for whoever's turn it is to do the pulling).

A similar activity is hiding under a blanket with your baby and making the outside world disappear. Providing you keep the game safe, as always, this can be a very exciting experience which combines babies' love of small, fitted spaces with their interest in watching things appear and disappear. However, make sure you are always with them under the blanket – your baby could become quite upset if you cover yourself up completely without including them and, vice versa, it could be too scary for them to sit on their own in this enclosed space without being able to see you.

You can exploit your baby's inclination towards tight spaces with all the variations of crawling-through-pipes that you can find in shops or create yourself. In the beginning your baby might need to see you at the other end in order to feel bold enough to venture in but eventually they will just sneak inside and loiter around the middle, leaving you wondering where they have got to when they do not reappear at the other end.

> **Tip:** There are many different ways in which you can hold your baby to make them feel safe, protected and supported by a strong bond of affection and love. Although hugging them tightly is something you do instinctively, you can also make it part of an anticipation and surprise game or use it as the expected end of a chase.

Filling and emptying

Putting things in a container and taking them out is an activity to which many psychologists like to ascribe deeper meaning. 'Container' is used as a metaphor for the mind and 'containing' refers to managing our own and other people's powerful emotions in a way that doesn't play havoc with the situation we are in. To 'contain' is to take feelings in, keep them there, and let them out again in a thoughtful and non-disruptive manner.

You act as a container of your baby's feelings each time you are confronted with a strong emotion in them. If, for example, your baby is gripped by frustration at not being able to reach one of their toys, you can help to calm them rather than letting the emotion overwhelm them. However, if you become visibly affected by your baby's cries and get frustrated yourself, you will fail to contain their feelings and amplify them instead.

Another way in which we act as a container is a more physical one. When we eat we put various foods inside us, digest them and let them out. Some traditions and beliefs, such as the Hindu system of Ayurveda, put food and emotional experiences on the same level, treating them as things that can either nourish and sustain us or poison us. We can see this link between food and emotion in everyday life: if we need comfort we may crave chocolate; if we feel stressed or worn down we may seek a hot drink (or something stronger) to relax and unwind. Also, if we vomit it is not always due to physical reasons – it can also be caused by emotional indigestion (like the shock of witnessing something unbearable).

At this physical level it is even easier to see how a baby's activity of stuffing things into a container and subsequently removing them can be regarded as a metaphor for one of the most fundamental activities of life. It is not surprising that the fascination for this activity peaks in the second semester, when a baby's physical and emotional boundaries start to feel more real and present.

In terms of your baby's cognitive development, filling and emptying also has remarkable importance. Babies do not have the same concept of mass and volume as us and always look rather surprised when the whole contents of the juice bottle do not fit in their tiny cup. This is also why they confidently try to ram the biggest square box of their set into the tiniest round hole, or put a Barbie-sized jacket onto a giant teddy. The action of emptying is also a learning curve for your baby, as pouring the whole contents of a box out may have a different outcome to what they had anticipated (the subsequent mess on your living room floor may come as a great surprise to them).

Keeping your baby's toys neatly packed in various baskets, boxes and bags is useful; not just for keeping things tidy but also for creating new games, as your baby will enjoy inspecting each box and tipping it over to see what is inside. Putting toys back in their 'home' at the end of every play session can also become a game in itself, especially if you slow down to your baby's pace and add some interest to the activity.

Babies' cupboards or drawers are also a good and practical idea. While you can keep most cupboard doors and drawers in the house locked, you can leave one or two accessible, making sure that you only leave in there things which, though not proper toys, are safe for babies and toddlers to play and experiment with. These cupboards or drawers are most useful in the room you spend most time in, so if you cook on a daily basis and you need the baby to self-entertain to some degree at these times, you can easily create a special area for the kitchen. You can fill it with tins, old bank cards, vacuum-packed food, long-life milk, cloth napkins, tape, old mobile phones and any other safe items, together with a few of your baby's toys. Make sure you renovate the contents every now and then so that it doesn't lose its charm! As with the safe items for mouthing and touching (as described in Chapter Two), you will find that your baby likes discovering the properties of these safe objects, where they can apply their natural curiosity and indulge their instinct for packing and unpacking.

Playing with language

In this period of development, playing with language will have a similar effect on your baby as pulling faces did in the first six months of life. As babies now understand more and more of what you say to them it becomes possible to surprise and amuse them in a number of ways: inventing words, pulling funny faces as you speak, pronouncing well known words with a strange accent (it must be clear that you are joking – you don't want to create confusion!), talking in rhymes, whispering or even pretending to say a word but only moving your lips. This last version of the game will give you an insight into your baby's ability to correctly associate verbal sounds with the movements of your mouth – lip-reading. If you play this game with those common words that you use every day with your baby, you will see them moving their eyes towards the object your lips referred to, showing you that they know what you are talking about even if you didn't make a sound.

This game is similar to the baby slapstick comedy mentioned in Chapter Two, as the source of amusement is totally unsophisticated and has an element of surprise and silliness. However, to find it funny when somebody breaks the rules of standard conversation, you must be aware of what these rules are. You must have expectations that things will go in a certain direction to laugh at a sudden unexpected twist. Therefore, if your baby laughs at your buffoonery this is a good sign – it is an indication that a series of complex emotional, cognitive and social skills have matured. Unfortunately, the development of a baby's sense of humour can be undervalued, as many parents feel much more reassured by the display of more standard and measurable skills, such as their baby's first words. However, leading our children towards an appreciation of the amusing and unusual things in life is more useful and beneficial to them (and us) than showing them the plain and obvious facts of life, which they will naturally discover by themselves.

Be aware: Although playing tricks with the volume of your speech and the facial expressions which accompany words is fun, you should NOT attempt to do the same with facial expressions indicative of emotions. Do not pretend to be suddenly angry, sad or indifferent – babies are very sensitive to emotions and understand the difference between your states of mind. To play with their understanding of feelings is not fair and is likely to confuse them. If you experience mood swings or a sudden drop in cheerfulness, there is nothing wrong with that. As mentioned in the previous chapter, verbalising feelings can be useful and productive, helping your baby to make sense of what's happening.

> **The psychology:** Researcher Edward Tronick carried out a famous experiment in which he applied what is known as the 'still face' procedure. Mothers were instructed to suddenly, with no warning, go from a warm interaction to adopting a poker face. The experiment was done with babies between two and nine months of age and what Tronick discovered was that not only were the babies aware of the unexplained change in their mothers, but they were also noticeably upset by it, and did everything in their limited power to cheer their mummy up again.

Reading at 6–12 months

A question you may find yourself asking at this stage is how much your baby actually understands when you read to them. This varies greatly among children, but by the time they reach a year old babies typically understand many simple commands and a number of single words representing common objects. If you choose a book recounting a story (rather than a baby book where each page stands on its own) you cannot expect an understanding of sequences and logic, not even of the most basic kind. For your baby at this stage, the words telling the story are worlds in themselves! Each one is full of interest for your baby, standing alone rather than as pieces of a story. Although your baby can already make very simple associations between a picture and its name, the overall story that you tell is just a container for various sounds, pictures and feelings.

The issue of how much your baby understands when you read to them is not something you should worry about. Without trying to assess your baby's intelligence or development, you can let your baby gradually

 discover the world of books (their smell, their feel and their individual personalities) at their own pace and in the way which comes most naturally to them. It doesn't matter if your child enjoys their stories because when they are read to something else happens, like sitting on your lap, hearing your voice, watching you turn the pages and so on. These are all important side effects which will probably lead your baby to appreciate and enjoy the full reading experience later on.

Don't be surprised if your baby shows a preference for unattractive or uninteresting details, disregarding the flamboyant and colourful scenes which to us seem much more worthy of attention. My daughter used to get much more excited by the drawing of a scrawny grey cat napping under the moon than by the smiley happy face of the big bright moon over which a man was climbing.

Although you may not know what your baby understands, there are a couple of things you can do:

1. Pointing to the pictures while you say the words is the single most useful thing to do to involve babies and hold their attention. At this stage names must be connected to their corresponding images, and you pointing to the pictures helps your baby see that they go together. It is also much more fun to read with your baby, rather than simply reading to them. Babies are better as partners than they are as an audience (you may have noticed that sitting still while you do anything is an impossible ordeal for your baby). Also, by reading together with them you teach them to participate, rather than just watch. Bashing the book, turning the pages backwards, rushing through to the last picture, uttering constant interjections and even biting or licking the text are all signs of a healthy interest in literature!

2. As mentioned in 'Making Choices for Your Child', it is possible to test your baby's reactions to different books to see what they are most attracted to. Through a bit of trial and error, you may be able to tell if they are more or less interested in particular topics, sizes, shapes, colours, or materials.

3. Even at this early stage, books are a good night-time routine. Once your baby is ready for bed you can read through some of the books they like and keep one – always the same one – as your last, to signal that the time has come to switch off the light. You can choose one of the many stories which end with the hero sweetly falling asleep: your baby will very soon realise that they are meant to try and do the same.

Key points

- Reaching developmental milestones is very hard work and behind every little, seemingly ordinary achievement there is tireless commitment and effort.

- A supportive and loving presence at the baby's side is all that is required – you do not need to make everything easy or go the opposite way to give them extra challenges.

- There is no right or wrong way to approach your baby's first steps towards independence – what is important is asking yourself the questions which will help you to feel comfortable and confident in your own position.

- By acknowledging that your baby is upset, you do three important things: take them seriously (building their confidence); reduce the risk of other attention-seeking behaviours; get to know and learn about your baby.

- You can reduce your baby's demanding interferences by allowing them a full view of what is going on.

- To overcome a sense of not getting it right (which at this stage of your baby's development is unavoidable) you must keep in mind that what is important is the process of asking, wondering, and trying things out.

- What is truly useful is a toy or book that your baby really enjoys – this will be what they dedicate their attention to for longer periods of time. Also, valuing your child's tastes and inclinations may teach them the value and beauty of becoming their own person.

- Praise must not be an evaluation, but more like an approving and enthusiastic description of why you think your baby is doing well.

- Playing with your baby is about spending time together where neither you nor your baby feel there is anything to prove or anybody to please. This allows them to try out their developing skills in a more natural way.

- To put reasonable limits on your baby's explorations you must decide what you are going to allow and what you are going to ban. Set a few strong rules in the areas you regard as most important, rather than trying to limit a wide range of things. This helps you to be determined and firm, prevents you from feeling guilty about saying no and helps your baby to understand that when you say no you really mean it.

- Cause and effect games are your baby's version of scientific experiments. As long as safety precautions are in place, be as liberal as you want in letting them try out new things.

- Through your own interactions with your baby, you interpret their state of mind and reflect it back to them, with all the feelings, emotions or moods that they have consciously or unconsciously picked up.

- Babies and toddlers do not only observe and imitate when we ask them to, but are like powerful video recorders: switched on most of the time and able to store an unlimited amount of material.

- Newborns need a tightly fitted space around them in order to feel comfortable and safe.

- 'Containing' refers to managing our own and other people's powerful emotions in a way that doesn't play havoc with the situation we are in. To 'contain' is to take feelings in, keep them there, and let them out again in a thoughtful and non-disruptive manner.

- Filling and emptying has importance for your baby – keeping their toys in various baskets, boxes and bags creates new games, as your baby will enjoy inspecting each one and tipping it over to see what is inside.

- Create a 'safe' cupboard or drawer in the rooms you spend most time in, full of things your baby will love tinkering with.

- Leading our children towards an appreciation of the amusing and unusual things in life is more useful and beneficial than showing them the plain and obvious facts of life, which they will naturally discover by themselves.

- Don't worry about how much your baby understands when you read to them. Let them discover the world of books at their own pace, and in the way which comes most naturally to them.

Chapter Four

How Your Baby Can Help *You*

In this chapter I will explain how playing with your baby can be a life-enhancing experience, changing you in both the short and long term. These gains can easily be overlooked – you may not have considered how playing with your baby can benefit you as an individual, perhaps considering it to be solely for the development or pleasure of your child. However, if you let your child guide you and keep an attitude of curiosity, interest and respect for their point of view, you will soon see how your baby can lead you towards a series of your own developments. You will find yourself accessing resources that you didn't know you had, including creativity, intuition, foresight, patience, resilience, self-control (most of the time) and lovingness. You may also discover new weaknesses or vulnerabilities, but this is not without its advantage – by better knowing your weaknesses you will be better equipped to manage them.

Every moment you invest in your baby counts, but this doesn't mean you have to give everything up in order to become a great parent – in fact, it's quite the opposite. By taking care of yourself too, you are providing your child with a wonderful companion. And if you play like a baby, the arrival of parenthood won't make you feel old, but instead rejuvenated with the sense of wonder and possibility that you will share each day with your child.

Discover things about yourself

Like with most life experiences, receiving the responsibility of looking after a baby is going to change you. It is not so much that you become a different person; more that aspects of yourself which were buried come closer to the surface, while characteristics that you thought were the very core of your personality move into the background. What type of person you are – and how you feel about it – is subject to considerable change during the course of your life, according to the demands, rewards and challenges that are placed upon you by circumstances and events. Through playing with your baby you can recover parts of your early history by watching your baby busy at play, experiencing their growth by proxy. You then not only learn about child development, but understand much more about your own evolution into the adult you have become.

Be aware: The experience of playing with your baby is going to put you more in touch with your own childhood experiences and although this will open up opportunities, it can also open up old wounds. It may be that some of your needs were neglected in your early years, such as your right to a worry-free time or your entitlement to your caregiver's unconditional love and attention. When you then have your own baby, you will be more in touch with the pain deriving from these experiences, especially if you decide to do things differently from how your parents did them. When you then immerse yourself in playful interactions full of love and fun, giving your baby something you didn't have yourself, you may end up feeling angry and upset. But if you stick to your intention to give your baby the best you can, and if you let their needs sit at the top of your priorities, the darker feelings you have revived may not only subside, but be transformed, and your old wounds won't have the same impact on your life any longer.

When you become a parent it is likely that a number of your strengths will come into play; it could be kindness, patience, playfulness or resourcefulness. However, I also discovered that what I had always regarded as one of my weaknesses was not so bad when it came to taking care of a baby. Going through life at a slow pace, being fond of idle time and being quite unadventurous were suddenly no longer a problem, and I think my first baby rather enjoyed all the time spent lounging between the armchair, the kitchen and her play corner. My very low tendency to 'get into action' was also useful during cold and rainy days, when I didn't need an excuse to stay indoors.

Another pleasant discovery for me was that through dedicating most of my time and resources to my new baby, I eventually got round to looking after myself better than I ever did before having children. I started feeling that my happiness and good humour were quite precious as I could witness their clear influence on my babies' moods. I thought they deserved to have a sunny person looking after them and for the first time I conceived of spoiling myself. I also started thinking that a whim is worth following if it means you are going to be contented, and looking after yourself can be as pleasant as looking after somebody else. So don't feel guilty for taking care of yourself – your baby deserves to have you at your best!

Understand relationships

The early stages of development tend to revolve around establishing, managing and maintaining rapports. This is why I propose that you play like a baby not so much as a way of doing something, but more as a way of establishing a two-way relationship through a range of possible activities.

Think about an ordinary event, like you suddenly sneezing loudly and your baby responding with a burst of laughter. Their reaction would probably surprise you and you may pretend to sneeze a second time to carry on with the 'game'. From then on, you may continue to perform all the actions leading up to a sneeze and your baby will start gearing up for laughter knowing what is about to happen. This improvised play session works well because of the baby's developing ability to notice infrequent or unexpected events. Your child's security in your presence (they would not laugh with a stranger) allows them to draw amusement out of a surprise, while your pleasure at seeing your baby enjoying themselves makes you carry on with the pretend sneezing. This is clearly more about something happening between two people rather than an activity taking place. Without the baby's trust in you and your pleasure at watching them laugh there would be no game at all.

Simple games such as the one described above will eventually lead you towards a better understanding of partnership and working together for mutual happiness. Through approaching your baby like a partner rather than a learner or audience, it is possible to understand a great deal. Immersing yourself in a playful relationship of this nature can improve your abilities in many areas, including how to: negotiate and compromise, modify your expectations, try out new things and observe their effect, pick up on implicit suggestions, and prevent failures from disappointing you.

In order to strengthen your relationship with your baby, what they need from you is emotional empathy – your willingness and capacity to be in touch with their feelings and take them on board. Since a baby does not use logic or reasoning they rely heavily on emotions to guide them, attuning themselves to your reactions and using them as a guide to form their own judgement. It is through this process that they progressively refine their instincts and form a mind of their own. Because emotion is the most effective way to connect and communicate with your baby, this leads you to use your emotional brain to a larger degree than ever before. You become able to make predictions and anticipate their reactions using your intuition and gut feelings. Essentially, you do the same as they do: interpret signs and read their mind. Getting a stronger grip on how things work from a baby's perspective therefore refines your 'sixth sense' – something your reasoning and logic never helped you to do. Do not be surprised, then, when you find yourself reading people's minds – and getting it right!

Undoubtedly, the most life-changing relationship you will ever have is with your child, so it is understandable if you feel a little nervous about it. I remember just a few hours after my first daughter's birth I was sitting comfortably in a big and soft hospital armchair when suddenly the thought popped into my head that she might not like me. Initially I just brushed the thought off without giving it much importance. However, I later realised that I must have unconsciously nourished that feeling for some time, since in my preparations for giving birth I behaved as if I was getting ready for a first date. After my waters broke I was shouted at for wanting to have a shower and do up my hair (in the end I was not allowed) but I still managed to wear my husband's best shirt for labour. The hospital pictures taken the morning after the birth show a new baby with her eyes closed and a mum wearing a necklace, earrings and eyeliner with some seriously smart pyjamas. It was not, as some friends jokingly pointed out, my Italian

obsession with looks; it was about doing myself up to meet a terribly important new person – one I initially felt rather intimidated by. The core of my main weakness – wanting to please others and fearing their negative judgement – had been touched within hours of my daughter's birth, and she hadn't said a word.

Invest in your family's future

Despite the much-advertised positive effects interactive play can have on your baby's development, these advantages will not be immediately visible to you. This could lead you to question the value of your input, wondering if your hours playing with a small baby are well spent or if they would be better spent elsewhere, on all the other things that need doing. Playing with your baby can be time-consuming and it may not seem the easiest option at a time when your workload is increased by the demands that parenting can bring. Some parents, therefore, prefer to encourage their babies to be independent, getting them used to sitting, playing and sleeping on their own from day one. However, growing evidence suggests that a baby's interaction with the main carer in the early years develops their brain, intelligence and capacity to manage emotions.

Through playing with your baby you show them how to go about entertaining themselves further down the line, using different objects, exploring the environment and having fun. The things you do together at this early stage make it likely that your baby will then become quite good at doing the same things when they are on their own or with other children as they get older. Their positive experiences of play and interaction with you will act as a powerful internal resource as they mature and the time you invested at the beginning will then really start to show. It is not an exaggeration to say that every second, minute and hour of your time spent talking, playing and interacting with your baby will be paid back to you hundredfold in terms of time and worries saved in the future, leading to better personal and family health.

Investing your time in this way drastically reduces the chances of behavioural difficulties in the future. Clinical psychologist David Coleman from the TV series *Families in Trouble*, provocatively points out that contented children seldom have behavioural problems. This is certainly true and, in addition, the more time you spend with your baby in a relaxed and informal way, the more likely it is that you will get to know their tastes, vulnerabilities and habits and will therefore be in a better position to meet their overall needs. Your child will then be likely to turn to you for help and guidance, as playing together does a lot to promote bonding. In my private practice, when a child manifests problems which may be related to receiving too little attention/consideration, I always prescribe 'play sessions' – a slot of time that is free of work, chores or lectures, to be dedicated to anything which might feed a shared interest or pleasure.

Take up new hobbies

Whenever something in your life changes, new possibilities open up to you. You may want to fight this and fiercely insist on sticking to the lifestyle you led before you became a parent, only with the added benefit or burden of new baby duties. On the other hand, you may feel as though you have to give up everything you've ever enjoyed and won't have any time for yourself until your child is old enough to attend school (or beyond). Both of these viewpoints are understandable but you don't have to hold either of them. If you are able to rearrange your priorities to adapt to your baby's rhythms and physical needs you will make room for other changes to follow – potentially rather exciting and fulfilling ones.

For example, think about giving up your nights out, your cycling holidays or your art classes, just for a while. You could then try to substitute these activities with something more compatible with your new parental duties, including things you had always been meaning to do but never got round to. You might start keeping a diary or corresponding with a distant friend, or, like me, discover classical music. Instead of those cycling holidays you might discover a fondness for strolling around countryside villages, or you may find painting at home more relaxing (and less expensive) than your art class. By seeing this as exchanging hobbies rather than abandoning them, you will also be likely to conceive new ideas and projects for the future, which may go from scribbles on scraps of paper to a finished novel.

Reshuffling your priorities to be with your baby and watch them grow affords you time to think and gives you a new space for reflection – a rare luxury which can change your life. Of course, turning a new page

by entering a different realm of experience can also be quite scary and it is certainly the ultimate nightmare for anyone who relishes being in control or is frightened of change. However, I am convinced that taking the plunge and letting yourself be guided through the day by the needs, character and will of your new baby is going to bring you closer to happiness.

Manage your time effectively

I remember how pleased I was when we were required to undertake a time-management course at work – I was thrilled by the thought of learning how to stop putting things off until the last minute. As well as being a waste of energy, postponing commitments and trying to forget about your agenda can spoil your free time, making you feel like you shouldn't be relaxing when there is still so much to do.

The key to time management is to prioritise your to-do list by splitting it into three different slots according to the level of urgency. You can do this by putting three to-do trays on your desk, labelled A, B and C (at home you could use three different sticky notes, or similar). In the top tray you file your A tasks, or urgent chores: those that cannot or should not wait until tomorrow. In the middle one you file your B tasks: those tasks over which you can take a little more time to think. And in the bottom tray, you file your C tasks: the more long-term projects and deadlines. An ideal working day should be made mostly of attending to your B tray, with your A tray being emptied quickly and your C tray being attended to in due course, with some of your long-term plans being transformed into actions as they take a clearer form. Isn't it simple! My problem with this strategy was that, being rather anxious, I tended to see everything as a top priority and worried about the consequences of postponing my C tasks as much as my A tasks.

It was only after I had my first baby that I started to forget about a lot of the less important things that I 'should do' and 'ought to have done', gradually realising that some things just don't make a difference to your life or other people's. I began to feel free of those niggling irrelevancies and became more enthusiastic about the things that do make a difference. As a result, my time management became much better, as well as my satisfaction with daily life.

The key to spending happier time is to put 'baby time' at the very top, in your A tray, knowing that whenever you can be next to your baby in a relaxed way – even if you're not doing much – you are actually accomplishing something valuable, even if little spare time is left for other commitments. Don't worry if your standards at home have become more relaxed – the rest of your family will enjoy your good mood far more than they would appreciate a tidy home. 'Baby time' and 'family time' belong in your A tray and other projects or duties will have to be dealt with from their B and C positions. This attitude can lead you to feel happier and more content.

Surprisingly, perhaps, this attitude can also help you to achieve more. A colleague of mine once told me that after having her first baby she had become terribly good at working from home. She explained to me how she had learnt to use all the small stretches of time that her baby allowed her, getting things done more efficiently than ever before. Knowing that a bare half hour could be all she had in a day, she used every second of it in the best way possible – with remarkable results. I must admit that it was only after I had a similar experience that I truly believed her. Initially I was rather sceptical about the idea that a baby could render you more efficient and organised, but I gave her the benefit of the doubt and started using my baby's afternoon nap as the allotted time for writing and preparing lessons. I was pleasantly surprised by the results and came to realise that looking after a baby can make you better at managing and appreciating the time you decide to set aside as truly yours.

Indulge curiosity

To learn an impressive amount from your baby's curiosity you just need to pay them attention. What is your baby looking at? Why are they flapping their hands? What made them smile? By letting your baby's eyes guide your own, you stop looking at things from an adult perspective and start noticing what interests your baby instead. In doing so, you change the normal focus of your concentration so that new or different aspects of your surroundings get your attention. You then realise just how much there is for you to still discover!

Through wanting to name what my baby's eyes were seeing (the most natural game parents play when they excitedly point things out to their children), I had to admit to myself that I could not tell the difference between a duck and a goose, let alone a coot. I also realised that my horticultural competence did not go much beyond roses and daffodils and that I did not possess any name for a small bird other than sparrow or robin. It is frustrating and rather embarrassing to turn to your baby with enthusiasm, only to say, 'Look at that lovely…bird!'

As I was walking to work one morning I overheard a snippet of conversation between a little boy (he must have been six or seven) and his mother. It went more or less like this: The little boy asked, 'Mum, how do they make croissants?' The mother replied: 'They just come out that way.' Then silence.

In all fairness, there are few people who know how croissants are made! However, a reply like the one above only served to make him quiet (which perhaps was the idea), frustrating his curiosity and desire to learn. If you are rushing around in the early hours of the day, thinking about what you have to do, you might not appreciate these kinds of questions from your child. However, when your child asks you a question you don't know the answer to, here are the things you can do to avoid dampening their curiosity:

1. Every child has the right to a bit of magic in their life so if you have the energy to invent something, do! Perhaps you had heard that croissants were invented by a man who could not get the moon for his daughter and invented a moon-shaped pastry for her.

2. If eight o'clock in the morning is too early to make things up, say that you don't know the answer but it's a good question. You could suggest looking it up on the Internet together or asking someone who may know the answer. You could even visit your bakery and ask them to show you and your child how croissants are made. Passion and interest, out of which happy lives are made, are often born this way.

So remember, only two conditions must be fulfilled in order for a baby's curiosity to benefit you. Firstly, you must assume that your baby's spontaneous enquiries, which they make by looking, smelling, touching, mouthing, grabbing, throwing and so on, are worth attending to. If you don't feel that way, your baby's curiosity will bother you for the workload it generates. The second thing you need is a modicum of courage and honesty to own up to the limits of your current knowledge. If you dare to confront these limitations and see yourself as someone who is still learning all the time, you will be drawn to an infinite range of new questions and will be on your way to becoming considerably more knowledgeable and wise. Let your baby be your teacher!

Develop your creative side

Every artist, writer or musician has faced the nightmare of a creative block. However, this can affect all of us, regardless of how seemingly creative we are. Whenever you try something new, for which step-by-step instructions don't exist, you are likely to find yourself in a similar spot: frustrated, disappointed, and unhappy with the state of things yet unable to bring about any improvement. You feel unskilled and ineffective. What do you do? With your baby, you can't drop out. You can get someone to babysit while you go shopping for a few hours but this will only provide temporary relief – you will still have to tackle the same issues at a different time. Playing with a baby day after day should teach you better than army training that surrender is not an option!

However, if you stick to your determination to see a problem through, you will eventually reach a more or less satisfactory outcome and, however taxing and exhausting the process, you will feel all the better for it. You are likely to invent some of your best games in desperation, when you feel you've run out of resources and decide that there is no way forward other than to make the most of a bad situation. Creative solutions are often born out of tricky times, as it is when the 'tension' rises that you learn new ways of adapting, twisting, juggling, improvising, and so on.

Holding a baby, soothing them and talking to them can often require you to invent something new, as a universal script does not exist. Baby talk leads you to create new words and sounds as well as new expressions; you also develop your imagination, spending time wondering how this new life before you is going to unfold. Don't expect yourself to be wildly creative straight away – if you find it a bit awkward at first this does not mean you are 'not good with babies'. It is important to remember that, like with anything new and challenging, you have to give yourself time and build up some experience before you can come up with creative ideas that work. If you don't let the initial difficulties discourage you, you will notice how you problem-solve, suggest, negotiate, and invent all the time when apparently you are only playing.

Another fundamental aspect of creativity is a certain bold disregard for the outcome of your productions, be it for a food dish you've invented, a watercolour, a poem or a jumper you've knitted from a pattern of your own. Creativity thrives within this lack of concern about external evaluations – the moment you start looking at your activities with judgemental eyes you inhibit the free flow of your ideas. Babies don't evaluate the quality of what they do and neither should you – the end product of your labour should not be used to measure whether you have been creative or not. Luck and chance are often the main forces behind successful creative solutions, which at other times may also come from genuine mistakes – the standard procedure gone wrong.

A concept which helps us to understand how creative solutions can come about (or be blocked) is 'functional fixedness', also referred to as 'mechanisation of thought'. This means that your thinking becomes functionally fixed – it loses its creative potential whenever you can think of an object only in relation to its most common purpose (i.e. scissors are for cutting, hammers are for nailing, etc.) even when a different use would solve a problem or come in handy.

So how can playing with your baby help you to become more creative in your problem-solving? It's quite simple: a baby has yet to learn the conventional use of things. In fact, quite the opposite is true – before being satisfied that a spoon is for eating with, they will have used it as a drumstick, a lolly, a sword and a gum teaser.

The psychology: Consider the following challenge, engineered by the German psychologist Karl Duncker in 1945. You are in a room and the only things you have at your disposal are a candle, a box of matches, a lighter, a hammer and some nails. Your challenge is to attach the candle to the wall of the laboratory in such a way that the wax will not drip on the table below. Can you see the solution?

When the experiment was first carried out, hardly anyone realised that they could have solved the problem by using the box in which the matches were kept – used as a small shelf to be attached to the wall with the nails as a support for the candle. However, when the experiment was repeated in a slightly different way and the matches were given out separately from their box, many more people arrived at the solution, being in a better position to think of the matchbox not only as a container for matches but also as an object with other useful purposes.

Paying attention to your baby's actions can help to lift you from the conventional way of seeing things and the mental ruts that we are all in as adults. This relates to the term 'lateral thinking', coined by Edward de Bono in 1967. Lateral thinking takes place when your flow of ideas is regulated not only by traditional step-by-step logic but by unusual or unorthodox associations as well, such as those you normally use when you tackle a brain teaser. The following riddle, for example, can only be solved if you look at it from an unusual angle: You can take away the whole and still have some left. You can take away some and still have the whole left. What is it? If you start picturing small and large particles, percentages, increasing and decreasing quantities and wholes of various dimensions and nature, you will be lead astray, as I was. The solution is incredibly simple and yet difficult to find, for it requires you to stop imagining various objects and think laterally to reach the word 'wholesome'. So, when your manager or someone else from the top of their ivory tower asks you to 'think laterally', they want you to take a side road or an unusual path in order to arrive at a solution – one they are not able to find themselves.

Feel young again!

In many cases, expecting and then having a baby is accompanied by the fear of losing the things you used to have and enjoy. You may be afraid of losing your free time, your figure, your social contacts and the freedom to do what you want with your life. That is why some parents cultivate a determination not to let their children impact on their lives and desperately try to carry on as before. If you share this view, you should keep in mind that the only effective way to prevent your children from changing your life is to not have them. The benefits of having children are less apparent if you make them fit into your elaborate schedules, but they become much more tangible if you let them take up the space they naturally claim in your mind and your agenda.

Many people believe that babies are definitely not the thing you need to counteract the effects of ageing. However, I believe this is a misconception. The first time that I ever had an unsettling sense of 'getting on' was on my thirtieth birthday. Although I had no specific worry, for the first time it wasn't just a celebration but an occasion accompanied by the foreboding that I was on the way to getting older.

This unease at having already gone through quite a chunk of my life lingered until I had my first child, Lucia. She arrived just as I turned 35, and at this point I started feeling as if a new life had just begun for me; that I was only at the beginning of something novel and exciting. I started having new thoughts, ideas, prospects and curiosities, wanting to know more about things in my surroundings. To counteract the typical sense of isolation and limitation in freedom of movement that comes with having a newborn in the house, I became a fan of new radio programmes, discovering how some classical music can be more soothing than a Turkish bath. I became fonder of visual art (admiring reproductions, of course – galleries have been off limits for a while) and discovered, to my surprise, that emotions and passion can be a quicker path to rational understanding than intellect or intelligence. In other words, I started to feel a bit like a baby myself: taking pleasure in discovery, exploration and learning, while leaving practicalities behind.

Wouldn't it be interesting, I thought one day, to add some bright colours to my grey/brown/black wardrobe; and why not indeed, some pink glasses to match my baby's outfit? I also started to write – no longer for psychology journals, but for myself, and no longer out of a sense of duty but for my own pleasure.

Playing with your baby is only the beginning of a long journey that will see you going from playing peek-a-boo when your child is eight months old to listening for hours when, at fourteen, she thinks she is not pretty enough. Spending what feels like hours helping her to choose a suitable outfit may then remind you of the days in which you repeated the same old silly trick over and over again, just for the pleasure of seeing her smile.

Key points

- You can recover parts of your early history by watching your baby busy at play. You then not only learn about child development, but understand much more about your own evolution into the adult you have become.

- Traits you may have previously regarded as weaknesses could now be strengths, e.g. enjoying idle time.

- You don't need to feel guilty for taking care of yourself – your baby deserves to have you at your best!

- Approach your baby like a partner. Immersing yourself in a playful relationship of this nature can improve your abilities in many areas, including how to: negotiate and compromise, modify your expectations, try out new things and observe their effect, pick up on implicit suggestions, and prevent failures from disappointing you.

- Getting a stronger grip on how things work from a baby's perspective refines your 'sixth sense'.

- Don't worry if you feel a bit nervous about getting to know your baby – you are bound to be anxious at the arrival of such an important person!

- Positive experiences of play and interaction with your baby will act as a powerful internal resource for them as they mature – the time you invested at the beginning will then really start to show. Every second, minute and hour of your time spent talking, playing and interacting with your baby will be paid back to you hundredfold in terms of time and worries saved in the future, leading to better personal and family health.

- The more time you spend with your baby in a relaxed and informal way, the more likely it is that you will get to know their tastes, vulnerabilities and habits and will therefore be in a better position to meet their overall needs. Your child will then be likely to turn to you for help and guidance, as playing together does a lot to promote bonding. This also reduces the chance of behavioural difficulties in the future.

- Consider substituting some of your old activities with something more compatible with your new parental duties. If you are able to rearrange your priorities to adapt to your baby's rhythms and physical needs you will make room for other changes to follow – potentially rather exciting and fulfilling ones.

- Put 'baby time' in your A tray! Know that whenever you can be next to your baby in a relaxed way – even if you're not doing much – you are actually accomplishing something valuable, even if little spare time is left for other commitments. Remember, the rest of your family will enjoy your good mood far more than they would appreciate a tidy home.

- Looking after a baby can make you better at managing and appreciating the time you decide to set aside as truly yours.

- When your child asks you a question you don't know the answer to, invent an interesting answer or tell them it's a good question and resolve to find out the answer later on.

- If you dare to confront your limitations and see yourself as someone who is still learning all the time, you will be drawn to an infinite range of new questions and will be on your way to becoming considerably more knowledgeable and wise.

- If you stick to your determination to see a problem through, you will eventually reach a satisfactory outcome and, however taxing and exhausting the process, you will feel all the better for it.

- Remember that with anything new and challenging, you have to give yourself time and build up some experience before you can come up with creative ideas that work.

- Creativity thrives when you don't worry about the end product – the moment you start looking at your activities with judgemental eyes you inhibit the free flow of your ideas.

- Paying attention to your baby's actions can help to lift you from the conventional way of seeing things and the mental ruts that we are all in as adults. Think laterally!

- The benefits of having children won't be as apparent if you make them fit into your elaborate schedules. Let your baby take up the space they naturally claim in your mind and your agenda.

Appendix:

Baby Psychology 101

Until recently, babies were seen as fairly incompetent. They were believed to be mostly unaware of their surroundings, deemed unable to make sense of their environment or the people in it. A baby's smile was often interpreted as a sign that they were passing wind; their intent gaze merely an indication of how they are wrapped up in their own world. Recent discoveries, however, point to the opposite fact: that although a baby's understanding must occur through different pathways and bear a different quality to our own, a baby is certainly not unaware, nor are they wrapped up in themselves. They are also not visually or acoustically impaired, as was once thought. In fact, all the babies that have taken part in psychological experiments have demonstrated that their vision is sharp, their hearing is accurate, their social skills are honed and their sixth sense is in better shape than ours.

The studies in this appendix are not just for academics, I promise! Through learning a bit more about baby psychology, I hope your understanding of their world and their amazing capabilities will increase even further.

The visual preference method

The pioneering of this method coincides with the beginning of infant research and can be traced back to the work of Robert Fantz, in the 1960s. Fantz had one of those outstandingly good ideas which, with hindsight, appear so simple and straightforward that you wonder why nobody thought of it before. He wanted to observe whether babies preferred to look at certain objects compared to others – this would establish whether they could tell the difference between the two.

Through his studies Fantz demonstrated that babies prefer faces over anything else in their environment. When a face-like pattern was presented next to something else it was always the face-like item that babies preferred, regardless of how colourful and attractive the other stimuli were. He also discovered that it is the typical geometry of the human face that babies respond to – if the same features (eyes, nose and mouth within an oval) are arranged in a random pattern they lose all their fascination with it. Perhaps this is not so surprising when you consider that a baby's life is totally dependent on human care and nothing can substitute it.

Babies also prefer:

- Curved lines over straight lines

- High-contrast images over softer ones

- Biological shapes over geometric or artificial ones

You can easily observe the visual preference method at home with your baby by putting two things in front of them; one slightly to their right and one to their left. If your baby cannot tell them apart they will either look at them indifferently or simply look in their favourite direction. On the other hand, if your baby looks at one of the two objects consistently more, even after you change its position, you will know for sure that their eyes are already capable of seeing a difference and that they have a definite preference.

The habituation method

There is another way to see if your baby can tell the difference between similar objects – it is called the 'habituation method'. This method can also tell you if your baby is interested in something or if they have become fed up with it. This 'game' is very simple and it is based on the fact that babies, like us, are attracted to novelty.

The habituation method consists of two phases. Initially an object is presented to the infant repeatedly until their interest has subsided and the visual scanning time has gone down to a baseline level (in other words, until they get bored with it and stop looking at it). At this point a new object is presented; one which differs in some way from the one they have become familiar with. If the baby's visual scanning time goes up again – their interest is re-activated – it means that they have noticed the difference between the two objects and are busy exploring the new one. This straightforward, yet convincing method has been extensively used to test the accuracy of infants' vision, disproving the claim that babies can't see colours and that they can only see in two dimensions.

Using the same method, Renee Baillargeon demonstrated that at three months of age babies are able to tell that something is amiss when they witness an impossible event, such as a solid figure shown to move through another solid. During these experiments the babies' level of attention rose much more when they saw impossible events rather than usual, logical happenings. Not only did they look at impossible scenes for longer periods but their heart rate also increased, suggesting that they felt a sort of surprise – as if what they were seeing shouldn't really be taking place. Even without scientific knowledge and with no previous experience of those scenes, babies were somehow able to read them correctly, identifying which ones followed the laws of physics.

Recognising sounds

Successful experiments with extremely young babies are not that common in infant research. One notable exception is that of Max Wertheimer, the famous German psychologist who, over 80 years ago, tested his newborn baby only eight minutes after his birth. He found that if you click your fingers by one side of the baby's head he will turn his head in the right direction, as if wanting to look at the source of the noise. It would therefore seem that we come into this world well-equipped by nature to accurately coordinate what we see and what we hear. The advantage for survival is obvious – you need to run in the right direction, away from any danger you hear approaching. Our species may not have survived if, at the roar of a herd of buffaloes getting nearer, we had to wait to check with our eyes to know which way they were coming!

In the last 20 years more and more evidence has been collected which demonstrates that our senses are well coordinated from birth. In another experiment babies were presented with two rattles which looked identical, but only one made a noise. The researchers wanted to see if babies could be deceived by the fact that only one of them produced the sound. Contrary to what one may expect, even young babies could tell which rattle was a fake and ignored it, preferring to focus their attention on the real one. They could therefore tell accurately which one was the source of the interesting sound.

By the time your baby is three months old they will already be quite sophisticated. They will be able to recognise familiar voices and familiar faces, tell where the voices are coming from, and even match a voice to its face. When babies hear their mother's or father's voice from a loudspeaker, with both parents in front of them, they direct their gaze to the person whose voice is being played, indicating that they can identify a face-voice correspondence.

Even more surprisingly, at four months babies are able to match a person's lip movements to the right vowels – they are essentially lip-reading. In an experiment, just like at the cinema, babies could watch faces on a screen while different sounds were played, mainly 'ah' and 'ee'. While in some cases the sounds corresponded to what the person on screen was actually saying, in other cases they did not match (like in a badly dubbed movie). The babies noticeably and consistently ignored the 'incongruent' speaker and directed their attention to the faces whose lip movements actually corresponded to the sounds they heard.

The dummy recorder

You may have noticed while feeding your baby that if you happen to feel inspired and start humming a tune, they stop feeding to look at you. The reason for this behaviour is that babies, like adults, have a limited set of resources and limited capacity to carry out more than one activity at a time.

When a baby's attention is engaged by visual or acoustic stimuli their sucking activity slows down. This very straightforward fact – babies stop sucking in order to listen to or look at something interesting happening around them – has been exploited by infant researchers, who found that babies hold back from sucking a dummy in order to hear their mother's voice but not a stranger's. These observations show that babies actually prefer listening to their mother's voice, in the same way that they prefer to look at her face, smell her smells and feel her touch.

Back in the seventies, Ilze Kalnins and Jerome Bruner studied how the sucking motion could be used by infants aged five to twelve weeks to cause a specific effect. These newborns were shown a colour film where the clarity/focus was dependent on them sucking an electronic dummy nipple. In one setting, called the 'suck-for-clear' condition, infants' sucking improved the clarity of the image, while in a second setting, called the 'suck-for-blur' condition, the opposite happened. Kalnins and Bruner found that the average rate of sucking increased significantly in the first condition, where infants had associated a pleasant effect with their sucking activity, and decreased significantly in the second condition. Furthermore, in the first condition the time spent looking at the picture increased too, whereas it did not in the 'suck-for-blur' condition. This research also highlighted how it is easier for infants to actively do something to achieve a result rather than to cease that action to achieve the same result (when the way to improve clarity was to stop sucking, the babies did not do so well). This study beautifully demonstrates how 'Please do this' is a more effective parenting strategy than 'Please don't do that.'

Recognising language

You may be surprised to learn that babies have the ability to recognise stories that have been read to them before they were born. In a famous study, twelve pregnant women were asked to read one particular passage from *The Cat in the Hat*. They were to do this twice a day for the final six weeks before their babies were due. Two to three days after birth, the method of recording infants' sucking, as previously described, was applied. It was found that babies slowed down their sucking rhythm in order to be able to hear the familiar passage of the story, while they did not do so when other parts of the story were being read. Interestingly, infants showed recognition for the story when it was read out by other female voices, indicating that it was the actual passage and not just the sound of the voice that they had learnt to distinguish. Further evidence of an early understanding of language is given by an experiment which showed that babies from English-speaking families are able to tell the difference between their mother tongue and a foreign language with different intonation characteristics (such as Japanese). They are able to do this as early as two months old!

Imitation

The famous psychologist Albert Bandura formulated one of the most well-known theories about imitation – the social learning theory – and demonstrated how this fundamental aspect of human and animal behaviour is a powerful engine behind learning and development.

Unfortunately, children are not selective as to what they are going to copycat – they will take up vices as well as virtues. In 1967 Bandura conducted an experiment which went down in the history of psychology as the 'Bashing Bobo Study'. In this study, researchers sat in front of a group of children and displayed an aggressive form of play; hitting, kicking and shouting at a big inflatable doll. These children were then observed to see how they would play compared to those who had had a non-aggressive play leader. Despite the relatively short time of exposure to the aggressive role model, the researchers found that aggressive play did increase when children had seen it being performed by the adult.

Friends and foes

When does a baby start to understand the more complex aspects of social interactions, such as the feelings underlying relationships between people or the intentions that motivate one's actions? Even in this area the findings have been surprising. At Yale University researchers demonstrated that six-month-old babies have a basic understanding of good and bad inclinations and are therefore able to predict who is likely to act as a friend or an enemy towards them. In a crucial experiment, babies were shown a scene where a character was trying to climb a hill. During the display he was either aided by a helpful character or hindered by an unhelpful one. The characters were represented by toys of different shapes and colours, all appealing to babies. When the time came for the baby to be free to reach out to one of the toys, all of the twelve babies reached out to touch the helper character rather than the nasty one. Babies therefore felt positive about the character who did good things and less positive about the one who behaved badly – something which has been discussed in relation to the early foundations of a sense of ethics and morality in children.

Working as a team

The Russian psychologist Lev Vygotsky introduced the idea of a Zone of Proximal Development: the gap between what a child can achieve alone and what they are capable of under the guidance of supportive adults or older children. When you hold a musical toy steady so that the baby can pull its string, the child is performing an action that they would not have managed on their own (they would have just pulled the toy along). In the encounter of two physical bodies and two minds, the actions performed are a product of the pair at work (or at play).

Influencing generations of child researchers, Vygotsky supported the view of development as essentially a social business and famously stated that, 'Every function in the child's cultural development appears twice: first, between people and then inside the child.'

There is also an American equivalent of this idea, introduced by Jerome Bruner in the 1950s – it's called Scaffolding. As you know, a scaffold is a temporary frame which allows access to otherwise inaccessible parts of a building, and it is in this very sense that the idea can be applied to education and play. The adult can act just like a frame, allowing the child to access otherwise unreachable meanings and actions until they start managing on their own, at which point the frame can be progressively withdrawn.

A dad's developing brain

Although we are unsure to what extent, it is possible to say that life experiences have a dramatic influence on all aspects of our bodily functions, including our genetic make-up – something which is not written in stone but subject to change during our lifetime.

Recording and measuring what happens in our brain when we perform a certain task is now relatively straightforward for researchers. They are able to tell us what parts of our brain are activated when we talk, dream, or solve a maths problem; they can also explain how people who extensively exercise a certain mental faculty, e.g. mathematicians, have more developed connections in the area of the brain which is home to that skill. Therefore, our brain physically changes in accordance with the demands that we place upon it. Like an athlete's body is shaped by exercise, the structure of our brain is modified through the actions we engage in, from reading to cycling to playing with a baby.

A recent study conducted at Princeton University looked at the effects of parenting on the brain of male marmosets. In this species it is in fact fathers who care for their infants; holding them, carrying them around, protecting them and handing them over to the mothers when they need feeding. The brain structures of these marmoset fathers were compared with male marmosets who had not fathered babies and the results showed that there was a marked increase in the neural connections in the frontal lobe of the brain of the fathers. The marmoset fathers' brains also had an increased number of receptors for vasopressin, a hormone that plays a role in caring behaviours and bonding. As the parenting experience causes the changes at brain level, these in turn support the fathers' activities and increase their aptitude at parenting, in the same way that exercising develops certain muscles which then support physical effort and make it easier. However, this doesn't just apply to marmosets! Being with babies modifies the chemistry of human fathers too, altering their levels of testosterone, prolactin and oxytocin, making their heart beat faster when they hear an infant cry.

Index

0–6 months 29–60
6–12 months 61–92

Abilities 10–11, 56, 64, 72, 74, 78–79, 82, 86–87, 91, 96, 113, 121
Action games 80, 96
Age 108–109
Anticipation games 45–46

Baby-talk 43, 105
Blame, avoiding 24–25
Body language 9, 42, 82
Bonding 18, 29, 99, 111, 121
Breastfeeding 32–33, 40, 44

Calming your baby 52–53, 55, 84, 105
Carrying your baby 34–35, 121
Cause and effect games 72–75, 91
Childhood, your 94
Colic 24, 33, 35, 52
Communicating:
You to baby 11, 12–13, 22, 41, 43, 97
Baby to you 31, 42, 79–80
Computer games 41

Crawling 61, 81–82, 83
Crying 23, 56, 63, 64, 72, 84
Creativity 7, 93, 105–108, 112
Criticism 15–16
Curiosity 12, 46, 61, 63, 65, 86, 103–104

Dad 121

Emergency play 65
Emotions
Yours 7, 13, 20, 23, 25, 58, 64, 84, 94, 105
Your baby's 9, 11–13, 25, 45, 48, 61, 63, 73, 79, 84, 87, 96, 98
Empathy 96
Encouraging your baby 68–69, 91
Entertainment
Yours to baby 18, 20, 21, 36, 43, 48, 49, 51, 52, 53, 58, 66, 68, 83
Baby's own 20, 72, 83, 86, 98
Exploring 31, 36–38, 62, 69, 72–75, 98, 115
Externalisation 24–25
Eye contact 9, 31, 76

Faces 45, 48–50, 76, 87, 114,
116–117
Failure and fear of failure 21, 22,
56, 68–70, 96, 110
Fear 18, 25, 45, 48, 73, 108
Feelings
Yours 7, 13, 20, 23, 25, 58, 64,
84, 94, 105
Your baby's 9, 11–13, 25, 45, 48,
61, 63, 73, 79, 84, 87, 96, 98
Filling and emptying games
84–85, 92
Frustration 24, 27, 52, 61, 68, 84

Gaining your baby's approval 22–23
Games 7, 18, 25, 29, 30, 38, 39,
42, 103, 105, 115
Action games 80, 96
Anticipation games 45–46
Cause and effect games 72–75,
91
Chasing games 81–82
Computer games 41
Emergency play 65
Filling and emptying games
84–85, 92
Housekeeping games 50–51
Naming game, the 40–41
Playing in small spaces 82–83

Playing with language 86–88
Presence and absence games
75–78
Getting to know your baby
18–19, 23, 32, 33, 38, 49, 64,
65, 89, 90, 99, 110, 111
Giving praise 68–69, 91

Happiness and success
Your baby's 14, 96
Yours 18, 95, 96, 100, 102
Hearing and listening 10, 43–45,
51, 58, 64, 109, 113, 116–117
Helping baby fall asleep 33, 35,
55–56, 90
Hobbies, gaining new 99–100
Housekeeping games 50–51
Hugging 32, 33, 84

Imitation 43, 78–81
Independence 15, 57, 61–62, 90,
98
Insecurity 13
Instincts
Your baby's 9, 11, 31, 38, 61,
68, 72, 79, 86, 97
Yours 19–20, 33, 84
Intimacy 58
Investing your time 98–99

Language development 10, 12,
26, 40, 42–43, 52, 60, 82,
86–87, 118
Laughter 22, 47–48, 72–73, 87, 96
Learning
Your baby 12, 21, 42, 43, 62,
66, 72, 76, 79, 85–86, 115,
119
You 93–95, 104, 109, 111
Loving your baby 14, 84, 94

Making choices for your child 66
Making judgements 15–16, 69,
70, 106, 112
Making mistakes 69, 76
Massaging your baby 33–34
Mouthing 37–39, 104
Mum 23, 43–45, 48, 64, 88, 97,
103
Music and dancing 57

Naming game, the 40–41
Nappy changing 33,34
Needing attention 16, 20–21,
64–65, 90, 99
Newborns 11, 36, 42, 50, 60, 61,
67, 83, 92, 109, 116–117
Observation
Yours 30–32, 94, 96, 110

Your baby's 35, 43, 48, 51, 65,
78, 89, 113–114
Parenting styles 56, 57, 62
Playing in small spaces 82–83
Playing like a baby 7, 14, 18, 21,
27, 29, 36, 38, 69
Playing with language 86–88
Playing without teaching 21–22
Presence and absence games 75–78
Progress 13, 26, 30, 35, 62, 66, 96

Reading to your baby 58, 67,
88–90

Safety 71, 73, 82, 91
Screaming 15, 29, 31, 56
Security 14, 96
Self-esteem 14, 64
Self-fulfilling prophecy 17
Sense of humour 87
Setting boundaries 70–71
Skills 7, 14, 22, 30, 61, 65, 67,
69, 72, 78–79,
Cognitive 87, 121
Emotional 82
Motor 39, 74, 82
Social 82, 87, 113
Singing 52–55
Sleep 33, 35, 55–57, 90, 98

Smiling 46, 50, 72

Social interaction 20, 45, 50, 119–120

Soiling 24

Songs 54–55

Sounds, recognising 41, 42, 43, 48, 49, 52, 82, 116–117, 118

Surprises, response to 47–48, 96

Taking care of yourself 93, 95, 110

Talking to your baby 10, 13, 23, 42–43, 51, 86, 98, 105, 110

Talents and gifts 14

Tantrums 63

Television 44

Throwing 40, 65, 72, 77, 104

Time and resources 7, 20–21, 61, 93, 95, 98–99, 105

Time management 101–102

Tone of voice 9, 23, 42

Touching

You 32–35, 47, 117

Your baby 39–40, 61, 74, 86, 104, 120

Understanding your baby 27, 63–65, 96

Watching your baby 30–32, 94, 96, 110

When things go wrong 24–25